THE COMPANY OF THE COMMITTED

The Company of the Committed

Elton Trueblood

PROFESSOR OF PHILOSOPHY
EARLHAM COLLEGE

HARPER & ROW, PUBLISHERS

SAN FRANCISCO

Cambridge		London
Hagerstown		Mexico City
Philadelphia		Sao Paolo
New York		Sydney

1817

To all the men and women who
belong to many denominations,
work at many occupations,
and live in many lands,
as members of one another,
because they sincerely desire
to wear Christ's Yoke with Him.

CONTENTS

PREFACE

This book is intended to represent the best thinking I can do on what seems to me a most urgent question, the question of how the Church of Jesus Christ can be so reconstructed as to play its potential role in the redemption of contemporary civilization.

The idea of the Church as a redemptive society has grown and developed in my own thought for many years. Though earlier efforts to deal with this theme are not duplicated in the present volume, they may reasonably be viewed as steps on the way. If any reader is interested in the progress of my own thought on the subject at hand publications are available. The first of these, written at the height of the great war and published in 1944, contained a chapter entitled "The Necessity of a Redemptive Society." The theme of the chapter was expanded later into a full length book, published in 1948, called *Alternative to Futility*. This book had an unexpected by-product in the formation of a loosely organized movement which, fortunately, crossed all denominational lines, and which continues to exist to this day, with many different names. I have learned a great deal from the thousands of dedicated Christians who have tried to produce new centers of vitality, not outside the Church, but *within* it. A third step, which marked growth in my own thinking, was the acceptance of the invitation to write, early in 1950, three articles for *Presbyterian Life*. The articles were entitled, "The Recovery of the Lost Provinces," "Recovery of Faith," and "The Order of the Carpenter." These were reprinted in a pamphlet sponsored by the American Baptist Home Missionary Society. Now, after eleven more years of thinking and learning and practical experimenting, with our situation really worse rather than better, I am ready to publish what I hope are mature conclusions regarding the urgently needed reformation of the Church in our time.

Perhaps it is only fair to say that I am a life-long member of the Religious Society of Friends. Though I value this heritage, it has been my intention never to let it cut me off from the life of the Church Universal. Since I was first introduced to it thirty-five years ago, I have accepted unconditionally the trenchant dictum of Samuel Taylor Coleridge: "He, who begins by loving Christianity better than Truth, will proceed by loving his own Sect or Church better than Christianity, and end in loving himself better than all." This explanation may help some readers to understand that my emphasis upon the essential Church as a militant order is not, for one of my background, a gratuitous paradox. I have made this emphasis for two reasons. First, the urgency of the time demands it; second, it is the emphasis of the New Testament.

It would not be right to conclude this preface without mentioning, for the first time in print, the great affection I feel for Eugene Exman, director of the Religious Books Department of Harper & Brothers. He accepted my first published book, twenty-five years ago, and he has been closely associated with the planning of all subsequent volumes.

The substance of this book was originally delivered as the Menno Simons Lectures at Bethel College, North Newton, Kansas, in 1960. Early in 1961 it was given as the Willson Lectures at McMurry College, Abilene, Texas, and as the Layne Lectures at the New Orleans Baptist Seminary.

E.T.

Earlham College
Easter, 1961

THE COMPANY OF THE COMMITTED

CHAPTER 1

The Necessity of Commitment

The restoration of the things that are wanting
The strengthening of the things that remain.
—Lancelot Andrewes

What reason is there to suppose that our civilization, in contrast to civilizations which have preceded it, will endure? The person who has not faced this question is hardly alive. That many different ways of life have flourished and have then declined is beyond contradiction. Consequently, there is no high probability that the fate of our civilization will be different—*unless*. The precise character of this "unless" is of such importance as to attract and to hold our best thinking, both individually and in groups. It is our most urgent question.

As we analyze the record of the experience of the past, we realize that neither technological nor material success is sufficient for endurance or even for survival. Life goes down, whatever the physical conditions may be, unless there is a relevant faith held by a sufficient number of the best minds. And not just any faith will suffice. It must have certain features, and it must be held with both intellectual integrity and dedication by self-conscious groups of people. Herein lies the crucial relevance of what we mean generally when we refer to the Church, since endurance requires both a spirit and a fellowship. Little is gained without the spirit, and the spirit cannot be maintained by separated individuals. Therefore the Church or somethng like it must be cherished, criticized, nourished, and reformed. The Church of Jesus Christ, with all its blemishes, its divisions, and its failures, remains our best hope of spiritual vitality. However poor it is, life without it is worse.

The paragraph above is a brief statement of a philosophy of civilization which has been elaborated elsewhere by many scholars and need not, therefore, be elaborated now. Suffice it to say that it is not absurd, that it can be defended with intellectual cogency, and that to the present author it seems true. Accordingly, in investigating our present predicament, we may proceed from this thesis on the assumption that it is a sound one. Assuming the necessity of the Church—or some similar society with an equally redemptive function—we need to ask fearlessly some penetrating questions about the existent Church. Has the salt lost its savor?

It is not likely that any valuable discussion of the possible alteration of the pattern of the Church's life will result unless we begin with a frank recognition of our relative failure. Strong Christian leaders—of whom Bishop James Pike of the Episcopal Church and Bishop Gerald Kennedy of the Methodist Church are outstanding examples—have had the courage in recent months to use the popular press to make our people realize that in large measure the contemporary Church is in retreat. Bishop Pike's remarkable essay on this subject, published in *Look* in December 1960, came as a surprise to many readers. They expected such an analysis from outsiders, but millions had failed to realize that the severest critics of the contemporary Church are the insiders who love her.

The seriousness of our plight is largely hidden from us because of certain marks of superficial success to which we can always point for comfort if we have any desire to do so. Thus, it is possible to take comfort in the fact that official church membership in the United States is higher than it has ever been in our entire history, whether we count absolutely or relatively. Membership is about three times as great *per capita* as it was at the time of the Civil War. In the second place, we can point to large budgets. A good many local congregations have budgets of more than one hundred thousand dollars a year, and these budgets are successfully underwritten. Some of our pride in this particular achievement is dimmed when we discover what a large proportion of the normal budget is devoted to the support of the local organization, particularly in the payment of salaries and the upkeep of local buildings—but in any case the budgets are large.

A third occasion for satisfaction is found in attendance records. The great attendance at public worship, long exhibited by Roman Catholics, is now generally matched by Protestants, the best success of this kind occurring in the southern parts of our country. Often the effectiveness of a clergyman is measured primarily by the crowds which he can attract, and by this standard some clergymen are highly successful. Of course there is always a strong possibility that the ease with which large crowds are gathered may not long continue. The United States is markedly different from the countries of northern Europe in this regard, and fashions have a way of moving west, so far as civilizations of European origin are concerned.

A fourth occasion of comfort is to be found in the contruction of new ecclesiastical buildings. In some communities the church which has not just completed a building campaign or is not about to start one is relatively rare. For the last few years we have spent in the neighborhood of one billion dollars a year on new physical structures for church purposes. Some of the new buildings are truly impressive and some are even beautiful, while nearly all represent genuine sacrifice on the part of numerous donors. It is important to recognize, however, that some of the motives for buildings are far removed from the motives of a redemptive society. In some areas the buildings minister to pride, and nearly all of them play some part in the ecclesiastical power struggle. Idolatry of the church building is one of the real dangers of our contemporary culture. The fact that the Church and the building are identified in popular speech is particularly disquieting. The point is more than semantic; it is indeed something of a revelation.

A more generalized feature of our society which obscures the relative failure of the Church is its public acceptance. We cannot normally have a public occasion, however secular, without religious representation. Thus, at President Kennedy's inauguration the committee in charge felt that it was wise or necessary to give public recognition, through vocal prayer, to four communions: Roman Catholic, Orthodox, Protestant, and Jewish. Furthermore, all four prayers were printed in *The New York Times*. This national recognition is only a consummation of what occurs at countless lower levels. In most communities leading clergymen are automatically invited to membership in the best luncheon clubs; ministers of all faiths are given reduced rates on the majority of railroads; and every church has the immense advantage of nontaxation of its physical property.

Before we take too much satisfaction from popular acceptance it may help our sense of historical balance to remember that the popular religion of ancient Greece succeeded in maintaining its shrines after the real vitality had departed. Representatives of Greek religion provided "services" long after what went on at the shrines had ceased to have any relevance in the life of business or education or government. It was to existent yet really obsolete shrines that the Apostle

Paul referred when he began his famous address at Athens by saying, "Men of Athens, I perceive that in every way you are very religious" (Acts 17:22).[1] They *were* religious; and their religion had some good features, as scholars like Gilbert Murray and Edith Hamilton have shown; but their religion died in spite of its assets. It died because it could not meet the tests of intellectual validity and social relevance; it could not match the new vitality of the fellowship which stemmed from the life and teaching and death and resurrection of Christ.

Many astute observers in our day are suggesting seriously that our Christian faith is now in essentially the same condition as that of the popular religion of Greece four centuries after Plato. Few have stated the danger more vividly than has Karl Heim, who compares the Church to a sinking ship:

The Church is like a ship on whose deck festivities are still kept up and glorious music is heard, while deep below the water-line a leak has been sprung and masses of water are pouring in, so that the vessel is settling hourly lower though the pumps are manned day and night.[2]

When we speak of the present sorrowful condition of the Church, we must be careful not to suggest that we are comparing our own day with that of a generation ago. In the last fifty years there have been some gains, particularly theological ones. No sensitive Christian can read Harry Emerson Fosdick's autobiography[3] without gratitude for the liberation from some debilitating forms of intellectual bondage which the majority of our ancestors experienced. What we must say is not that the condition of the Church is worse than

---

[1] Unless otherwise stated, all Biblical references are to the Revised Standard Version.

[2] Karl Heim, *Christian Faith and Natural Science* (New York: Harper & Brothers, 1957), p. 24.

[3] *The Living of These Days* (New York: Harper & Brothers, 1956).

it *was*—which may or may not be true— but rather that the Church is far weaker right now than it *might* be. Areas could be occupied which are now neglected; resources could be employed which are now wasted. The real problem before us is not whether our faith has declined, but how it can be made more truly relevant to contemporary life and its urgent needs. However good the contemporary Church is, it is not good enough; it is not so good as it might be, in view of its glorious founding and in view of its current unexploited resources. And its adversaries are strong.

The purpose of assessment is not to indulge in unproductive pathos or to boast of our undoubted successes. It is, instead, to give us such a clear understanding of where we are that we may be able to go forward, using powers which may otherwise be wasted. Realism and idealism are both needed and needed together. The defense of engagement in sober realism is always that without it there is no real possibility of idealistic advance in the future. Although there have been in the modern Church great gains as well as great losses, it is more profitable to stress the losses. For when we know what we face, we may see better how change can be produced. At least, by so doing, we avoid complacency. Our enduring faith is that of Ezekiel, that no matter how dry the bones may be, breath can come into them and they can *live*. This has been demonstrated many times in both Jewish and Christian history. When the great Timothy Dwight took over the presidency of Yale College not one student would admit publicly to faith in Christ. When Dwight ended the presidency twenty-two years later, in 1817, the entire intellectual climate of the college had changed: it changed because Dwight did something about it.

Christianity, as we know it in the West, appears in three major forms. The first of these is standard Protestantism, the dominant religious pattern in American civilization for three hundred years, though the dominance may already have ceased. The contemporary danger in this sector is dull conformity—neither hot nor cold but alarmingly tepid in the level of concern. Much of the effort goes into paying for buildings and keeping up the mechanics of the organizations. Because many of the most successful pastors are able promoters, the organization can go on for some time after the life has departed. Standard Protestantism is characteristically urbane and well-mannered, but it is sadly deficient in driving power and in the ability to imagine new and fresh ways of permeating the world. Alfred North Whitehead described, with characteristic frankness, the decline of Protestant effectiveness in words which all who care should ponder. "Its institutions," he said of Protestantism, "no longer direct the patterns of life."[4]

The second major strand in American religious life is Roman Catholicism. It has gained such great power, by virtue of both its numbers and its interior discipline, that membership in the Roman Catholic Church, far from being a political liability, is now an obvious asset and will probably continue to be so for a long time to come. The Roman Catholic Church has such a hold on a variety of minorities that it may easily become in our lifetime an effective majority. It has enough prestige and glitter to hold the loyalty of the impoverished and enough intellectual appeal to hold some educated persons. At the same time, however, it involves a terrible ultimate weakness in its totalitarian claims. It claims, officially, to be the only true Church, with the logical corollary that all other Christians are heretics. This is why the rule against worshiping with other Christians is enforced with such severity. Sharing in worship would be a tacit recognition of validity. In its claim to monopoly, and

[4]Alfred North Whitehead, *Adventures of Ideas* (New York: The Macmillan Company, 1933), p. 205.

in its parallel emphasis on its own spiritual prestige, the Roman Catholic Church runs exactly counter to the teachings of its supposed Founder who undermined all arrogance by washing the disciples' feet and countered all monopolistic claims by saying "other sheep have I which are not of this fold." The basis for the temporary strength of the Roman Catholic Church in the modern world will also be the basis for its ultimate faiiure to speak to the minds of more thoughtful men and women.

The third major strand in contemporary Christianity is that represented by the plethora of sects and fringe movements. These, known by many names, combine a truly impressive evangelical zeal with a theological fixation on a kind of Fundamentalism which cannot bear examination by critical minds. They are, on the whole, more nearly equal to the Communists in driving power than are either Roman Catholics or standard Protestants, and this one feature makes them impressive. Though their chief success is, for the most part, among people of relatively low income and of inferior educational opportunity, the commitment they secure is so great that the work done and the money contributed by their adherents are often greater than the corresponding work and giving of more privileged people. The outside observer, if he tries to be fair, is bound to be impressed with the level of dedication among these groups, though at the same time he is bound to be aware that this religion cannot win. What it lacks, fundamentally, is the full commitment of mental powers, without which a faith cannot be enduringly effective.

Much of our present tragedy lies in the fact that many who want to be part of Christ's cause cannot feel at home in any of the three major forms which the contemporary Church takes. They are looking for a bold fellowship, and what they find is a complacent society concerned to an absurd degree with its own internal politics or so unimaginative as to suggest that the world can be saved by three hymns and a sermon or a Mass. The needle seems to be stuck in a groove. Many contemporary seekers cannot abide the Church as they see it, their dissatisfaction arising not from the fact that membership demands too much, but rather from the fact that the demands are too small. It helps our humility to admit that some of the critics may be on the right track.

Though the three types just mentioned are the major choices now open to Christian men and women in the West, there are naturally many variations of the types and some which defy such classification. In addition to the three weaknesses of the three types, there is a general weakness which may be termed *segregation,* especially segregation from common life. Whether our religion is segregated from common life by being limited *geographically* (i.e., to a religious building), or *temporally* (by undue emphasis on one hour a week, which is usually on Sunday morning), or limited in *personnel* (by the assumption that religion is the responsibility of a special professional class called clergy), the damaging effect is the same.

When we think that religion is what goes on in a building of recognizable ecclesiastical architecture, the damage comes in the perfectly natural human tendency to minimize religion in *other* places. When we think of religion as what transpires on Sunday morning, the harm lies in the tendency to suppose that what goes on at other times, in factories and offices, is not equally religious. When we think of religion as the professional responsibility of priests, clergymen, and rabbis, the major harm lies in the consequent minimizing of the religious responsibility of *other* men and women. The harm of too much localizing of religious responsibility in a few—however dedicated they may be—is that it gives the rank and file a freedom from responsibility which they ought not to be able to enjoy.

The major danger of our contemporary religion, then, is that it makes small what ought to be large. By segregating religion in place or time or personnel, we make religion relatively trivial, concerned with only a part of experience when it ought to be concerned with the *whole* of life. Whenever the Church means merely a building on the corner, or a special kind of service, or a man with a round collar, the salt has already lost much of its savor. But there can be no serious doubt that for millions the Church *does* mean precisely that. It seems successful, but it is fundamentally unimportant because it is deemed to be marginal in its relevance. In so far as this is true, it is not only Church *members* but the *Church itself* which requires a radical conversion. Few phrases deserve currency in our time more than the phrase "The Conversion of the Church."

This phrase provides the real justification of the labor of writing books such as this. We have reason to believe that civilization cannot be redeemed without the Church as a redemptive society, but the disturbing thought, which must always be matched with this one, is that the Church as we know it is not now good enough to fulfill its redemptive function. The basic trouble is that the proposed cure has such a striking similarity to the disease. No one denomination has the perfect pattern and, furthermore, no church has the right to be proud. I do not know precisely what the true Church is, but I am certain that it is different from and better than *mine*. We do not seek a victory for any of the existing groups, as though Christianity were engaged in an internal power struggle. Indeed, it is important for us to realize that words like "Catholic," "Protestant," and "Evangelical" have become so ambiguous as to be virtually meaningless. Nor is mere union of the denominations our primary need if we are to have renewal. The movement we need is a movement in depth, and if it is deep enough the problem of unity will take care of itself. As lines go down vertically from the surface of the earth they necessarily come nearer to one another. In any case, the divided condition of the modern Church is by no means its greatest evil or weakness. We could stand division if we had genuine commitment to Christ and His cause.

Superficially, the Church appears to be riding high, but closer examination of the situation is disconcerting. Our position is not unlike that of the Roman Empire when it appeared to be at the height of its prestige, with great show of power at the center, but actually was losing province after province on the edges. Things looked very good in Rome, for example, after Britain could no longer be held. The contemporary lost provinces are indeed numerous, so far as the living Church is concerned, but three are especially disturbing. The first such province, requiring immediate attention, is that of higher education. Though originally, in our culture, most colleges and universities were instituted and supported and dominated by Christian conviction, this is far from true today. A few colleges have made bold steps to become consciously Christian in their total effort, seeking to build again on their earlier foundations before it is too late, but these are still a conspicuous minority. Even those institutions which still recognize their Christian origins are, in many ways, as secularized as are any others.

There is no way of knowing accurately how many students have any real commitment to the Christian cause—and it is certainly uncritical to pay much attention to the answers to questionnaires, in this or any other important field of experience—but it is not hard to see that Christian conviction has been eroded among students and professors. This is shown in many ways. An extreme example of the evidence is that a service of dedication on the World Day of Prayer, set up in a university of six thousand persons, and well advertised, brought an attendance of *five* students and no professors. Obviously, the whole thing seemed irrelevant to the students and their teachers. It did not have the urgency of a basketball game or a dance or even of a scientific discussion.

The denominational foundations which surround the chief campus areas do their best, but they touch, in most institutions, only a tiny minority. One knowledgeable observer who has visited many colleges has told us that perhaps two per cent of the more than three million students in the colleges and universities of the United States are deeply concerned and dedicated Christians of *any* variety. Many students, as well as great numbers of professors, are openly contemptuous. If professors think they will not be quoted, many will say quite simply that the Christian faith seems to them something which was perhaps useful long ago but is no longer relevant to modern society with its manifold issues, intellectual and otherwise.

The primary problem, it must be noted, is not usually one of explicit atheism. In some institutions of learning it is probable that the majority of students and a fair proportion of professors would admit rather reluctantly to some kind of belief in some kind of God, but this is not the point at issue. Since Christianity has never survived on the basis of mild and uncommitted theism, it is certainly not likely to survive on that basis today. Something more is required for victory, and it is the precise character of this additional element which we must make an effort to understand. In any case, when the Church is looking for a mission field it need not look beyond the nearest campus.

If the campus is largely a lost territory, so far as an unapologetic Christian faith is concerned, the same can be said of youth in general. The average church today has the loyalty of the small children and the support of the old people, but there is a conspicuous gap between these age groups. So far as attendance at public worship is significant, and it is partly though not wholly so, the absence of youth is obvious to any interested observer. Often in congregations of, say, two hundred persons it is impossible to find ten who are under twenty-five. The great loss begins in high school and continues, usually, until people are in their thirties. This partly accounts for the fact that so many genuine conversions come in middle life. People who have left the Church in youth sometimes come back to it with conviction when they are old enough to be deeply serious, both about themselves and their children, but others never return at all. They are lost to the life of the Church as young people and they remain lost.

A number of churches claim to have highly successful youth programs, but not all of these will bear close examination. What we discover is that the youth program in many local churches is almost entirely one of entertainment, not really different in kind from the secular entertainment which is provided in such abundance by those modern parents who strive pathetically to keep their children happy. The inequality of the sexes in Christian youth programs is also something to note with a sense of shock. It is not uncommon to listen to a youth choir in which the girls outnumber the boys five to one. Insofar as we care about the Christian cause we are bound to ask why this is so. Incidentally, it is not true of the Communist youth groups, which stress preparation for occupation of capitalist cultures rather than being temporarily happy.

A third lost territory is that of organized labor. Many committed Christians work with hand or brain, whether in offices or homes or on farms, but relatively few of the ranks of organized labor are to be found among those who are serious about the Christian cause. This is partly because labor union members often think that they have found a cause of their own which makes the Christian cause unnecessary.

They note, of course, that the majority of church workers appear to be of the owning and managerial class. Accordingly, the Church takes on more and more of a class structure. The historic American Protestant denominations suffer most severely in this way, the Roman Catholics and the Fundamentalists suffering a little less, but no group is doing really well in holding the imagination of organized labor.

What a paradox it is that the Church of Jesus Christ, the Worker, should seem alien to those who work with their hands! After all, He was called the Carpenter (Mark 6:3), and there is reason to suppose that He made both ox-yokes and plows in the carpenter shop of Nazareth. Historically, Christianity has glorified work and has given to the modern world the marvelous idea of *vocation*. The faith certainly has a potential contact with labor if only we are able to see how to employ it. In any case, however, we have lost ground, and this ground must somehow be recovered if the kingdom of Christ is to prevail. Some Christians are working at it with great dedication, but most of the lost territory is still to be occupied.

There is no doubt that the tide of secularism is rising. In Russia and in mainland China it is regnant or at least unchallenged. We have seen in these countries the fulfillment of the dire prediction of Dostoyevsky that the time would come when the greatest change was not that of a church becoming a state, as with the Vatican, but rather that of the state becoming a church.[5] That the latter danger has materialized is an insight which modern man will neglect at his peril. How else can we account for the entire tone of Prime Minister Khrushchev's speech of January 6, 1961? In that speech he was acting both as official philosopher and as high priest in showing the path which his conquering "church" must take.

[5] Fyodor Dostoyevsky, *The Brothers Karamazov*, Bk. II, Chap. V.

What worries us rightly in the West is not that the two major parts of the world are so different, but that they are coming to be so much alike. What is now emerging, it would seem, is not two radically different systems, but two variants of the same materialism. If we are inclined to dispute the existence of the materialism of the West, all that is required to convince us of its reality is a careful study of advertisements, particularly at Christmas time. In preparation for the birthday of Him who had not where to lay His head, we are urged to buy for the wife a forty-thousand-dollar necklace or, for a couple, matching airplanes marked His and Hers. Thousands of students celebrate Easter by an orgy of self-indulgence at Fort Lauderdale, Florida.

Succeeding generations, as they try to evaluate our culture, will not have much evidence that is conclusive about our religious life, but they will have abundant evidence by which to judge our manner of living. What will surely strike researchers as odd if they still have access to the words of the Gospels is that these words will seem to have had no effect at all upon the manifest cult of self-indulgence. The remaining pages of slick and expensive advertising will appear more of a revelation than will the seemingly obsolete words of Christ about losing one's life and identification with the poor and humble.

The test of the vitality of a religion is to be seen in its effect upon culture. The more we recognize the deep similarity between our own culture and that of imperial Rome, the more we see the significance of a great passage in the late Boris Pasternak's *Doctor Zhivago,* a passage which helps to explain why Pasternak's book has not yet been published in his own language in his own country. Our shame is that the new Rome is not equally challenged.

Rome was a flea market of borrowed gods and conquered peoples, a bargain basement on two floors, earth and heaven, a mass of filth convoluted in a triple knot as in an intestinal obstruction. Dacians, Herulians, Scythians, Sarmatians, Hyperboreans, heavy wheels without spokes, eyes sunk in fat, sodomy, double chins, illiterate emperors, fish fed on the flesh of learned slaves . . . all crammed into the passages of the Coliseum, and all wretched.

And then, into this tasteless heap of gold and marble He came, light and clothed in an aura, emphatically human, deliberately provincial, Galilean, and at that moment gods and nations ceased to be and man came into being—man the carpenter, man the plowman, man the shepherd with his flock of sheep at sunset, man who does not sound in the least proud, man thankfully celebrated in all the cradle songs of mothers and in all the picture galleries the world over.[6]

The outstanding success of the recent motion picture version of *Ben-Hur* was more revealing of our own culture than of the culture which was supposedly depicted on the screen. Both the battle at sea and the chariot race succeeded in exciting the viewers tremendously, but the religious scenes fell flat. Though *Ben-Hur* is subtitled "A Tale of the Christ," the representations of Christ's work were largely unconvincing. Almost all that the producers could think of to depict Christ's work was an assemblage on a hillside. This accurately indicates our own preoccupation with public meetings as the chief form which contemporary religious experience can take, but it was certainly not the chief form it took during the formation of the original Christian community. Then it was far more a matter of almost secret instruction of the small cell and the sending out of ordinary men two by two. But these operations would hardly be recognized as authentically Christian by modern movie audiences. Words like "take up your cross daily" seem quaint to a generation which is only mildly shocked by the advertisement of the solid gold putter.

[6] Boris Pasternak, *Doctor Zhivago* (New York: Pantheon Books Inc., 1958), p. 43.

It is hard to exaggerate the degree to which the modern Church seems irrelevant to modern man. The Church is looked upon as something to be neither seriously *fought* nor seriously *defended*. A church building is welcomed, partly because it provides such a nice place for a family wedding; and, after all, most families expect weddings, sooner or later. A church is also a good place to send the children on Sunday morning—they might learn something helpful, and certainly the experience of being sent will do them no harm. The point is that such conceptions are wholly consistent with the idea that the Church has only marginal relevance. We do not expect, for the most part, to find the gospel centered in a burning conviction which will make men and women change occupations, go to the end of the earth, alter the practices of governments, redirect culture, and remake civilization.

Some indication of the mildness of our religious conviction is illustrated by the fact that we spend more on dog food than we spend on foreign missions. Another indication is the fact that we expect the inaugural address to be more inspiring than the prayers which precede and follow it. In short, we welcome religion, but we expect it to be innocuous and, above all, unfanatical. We are willing to accept it, provided that it involves no zeal. It is at this point that the contrast between the mildness of our faith and the burning devotion of the Communist faith is so disturbing. If only we possessed another object of devotion as an alternative to that involved in Christianity the situation might be less disturbing, but there is no such devotion in sight. Certainly democracy as an article of faith does not elicit any transforming power, while only a minority is able to understand the connection between democracy and a transforming faith which makes democracy reasonable.

Most of the defection from the Church in contemporary life is not that of outright antagonism. Bitter denunciation

may be found among some college students and in some parts
of the labor movement, but most of the rejection of the
Church is far less vocal or self-conscious. What we face in
most areas of experience is merely the unexpressed assumption of men and women that the Church of Jesus Christ is
not in the least connected with what means most to them.
If they have a cause it is likely to be comparable to the cause
of the class-conscious laborer who believes with all his heart
that he is working for economic justice, but who never con-
nects his own deep concern with the Biblical message of the
Prophets of Israel or with the Church as he knows it. The
message of the Church, as he understands it, is not so much
untrue as irrelevant. In like manner, thousands of contemporary scientists and technologists see no connection,
logical or otherwise, between the central faith which inspires
the Church and the intellectual urge which drives them to
their work.

The only important exception to the general lack of connection between the Church and dominant concern is provided
by the Negro population of the South. Those who have
worked so intelligently and so bravely for equality of opportunity have tended to find the Church their rallying point.
This was conspicuously true in Montgomery, Alabama,
under the leadership of Martin Luther King, in the successful drive against racial discrimination in buses. If the drive
had had some other center, the resulting violence might have
been really frightful. It ought also to be recorded that,
cowardly as many congregations are, the major help given to
those in New Orleans who were persecuted for taking their
children to integrated schools came from the churches. Other
congregations paid the rent of the pastor whose original
home was attacked by mobs.

The paradox of the apparent victory, yet real defeat, of
the contemporary Church is nowhere more vividly demon-

strated than in the present concentration upon *attendance*. Great billboard advertisements appear by the hundreds with a single message, "Worship Together This Week." The fact that the donors of the advertisements are undoubtedly motivated by goodwill toward the life of religion, as they understand it, does not obscure the fundamental ineptitude of their effort. Obviously, the sponsors of the advertisements look upon attendance at a religious assembly as the major religious act or the major evidence of church membership. It is no wonder that they think this, if they observe the frantic and sometimes ingenious efforts of pastors, week by week, to surpass all previous records of attendance. The promotional purpose of local church newsletters is transparent.

The tragedy of the billboards lies less in what they say than in their revelation of a suppressed premise concerning the central nature of Christ's cause. Many betray the same unargued assumption when they describe themselves by announcing which church they go to. The trouble with this response is that a church, in its very nature, is not really something to which men and women can *go*. Rather, it is something which they may be *in*. The difference is fundamental and far-reaching. We can go to a railroad station or to a motion picture theater or to a ball game; but a church is something which demands a wholly different human relationship, the relationship of belonging. If a man is really in—really belongs to—a church, he is just as much a member of it when he sits at his desk in his business house as when he sits in a pew at his meetinghouse. The point is that the relationship, if real, is continuous, regardless of time and place and performance. Christians made a great step forward in human history when they took from Stoicism the germ of the membership idea and developed it.

The radical difference between the Church and most human

organizations is so important that unless it is truly understood our chance for renewal of vitality is slight indeed.
Though it is sad that people fail to respond to public
worship with the enthusiasm and devotion which they evince
at basketball games, the greater sadness lies in the fact that
supposed Church members do not even understand the difference between the two kinds of relationship. If Christianity
is primarily a matter of attendance at a performance, it is
not different in kind from a host of other experiences.
Though membership may *include* attendance at performances
of a certain character, such attendance is not the primary
meaning of the Christian effort at all. The fact that this is
not generally understood is one of the chief evidences of the
spiritual erosion which distresses us.

There are always some people who, in times of discourage-
ment or perplexity, cry out that what we need is religion.
The evidence of our time makes clear to us, if it was not
clear before, the essential ineptitude of such remarks. We
have religion; the problem is always the precise character of
the religion. We can apply now the lesson which Whitehead
taught so vividly in his Lowell Lectures—that religion, far
from being necessarily good, may be terribly evil. It may
produce bitterness; it may become a tool of the power
struggle; it may be purely instrumental, so far as the individual is concerned; it may descend into gross superstition.
"In considering religion," wrote Whitehead, "we should not
be obsessed by the idea of its necessary goodness. This is a
dangerous delusion. The point to notice is its transcendent importance; and the fact of its importance is abundantly made
evident by the appeal to history."[7] The widespread belief in
the necessary goodness of any and all religion, far from being
one of our assets, is one of our contemporary liabilities. It is

[7] Alfred North Whitehead, *Religion in the Making* (New York: The
Macmillan Company, 1927), p. 18.

part of the reason that we are not so disturbed as we ought to be. Only if we have a beneficent disturbance will we put real effort into trying to learn what the nature of the sorely needed faith is. Where, then, do we start if we mean to rebuild?

We all understand, when we give our minds carefully to the question, that to be an effective Christian it is not enough to be an individual believer. Inadequate as the fellowship of the Church may be, in many generations, including our own, there is not the slightest chance of Christian vitality without it. Apart from the poor and all too human fellowship called the Church we should not have had even the New Testament. Men are often brave and good alone, but they are never really effective unless they share in some kind of group reality. Voices crying in the wilderness are not permanently recorded. Furthermore, the indispensability of the Church is demonstrated by the fact that the new life normally arises from the inside. The ultimate evidence of the divine ordering of the Church is the way in which it is always the members of the Church itself who are the most intelligent critics of her life and witness.

The crucial question today is not whether we must have a fellowship, for on that point we are reasonably clear; the crucial question concerns the *character* of the fellowship. The more we think about it the more we realize that it must be a fellowship of the committed. This is because mere belief is never enough. Some writers and speakers give the impression that the main adversary we face is atheism, with the consequence that they try to convince other men that "there is a God." Although the philosophy of religion, including the case for theistic realism, is an important intellectual discipline and one which a true scholar will never neglect or even minimize, the chief barrier to a renewed vitality in the Christian society is not lack of belief. Millions who feel no sense of urgency about the Christian endeavor will list themselves, when inquiry is made, as believers of some sort.

There is no better way, in contemporary thought, of approaching the meaning of commitment than by reference to Marcel's distinction between "believing that," and "believing in."[8] To be committed is to believe *in*. Commitment, which includes belief but far transcends it, is determination of the total self to act upon conviction. Always and everywhere, as Blaise Pascal and many other thinkers have taught us,[9] it includes an element of wager. This is why in great religious literature, including the New Testament, the best light that can be thrown upon commitment is that provided by marriage. For everyone recognizes the degree to which marriage is a bold venture, undertaken without benefit of escape clauses. The essence of all religious marriage vows is their *unconditional* quality. A man takes a woman not, as in a contract, under certain specified conditions, but "for better, for worse; for richer, for poorer; in sickness and in health." Always, the commitment is unconditional and for life. The fact that some persons fail in this regard does not change the meaning of the glorious undertaking.

One way of stating the crucial difference between belief and commitment is to say that when commitment occurs there is attached to belief an "existential index" which changes its entire character. Belief *in* differs from belief *that*, in the way in which the entire self is involved. "If I believe in something," says Marcel, "it means that I place myself at the disposal of something, or again that I pledge myself fundamentally, and this pledge affects not only *what I have* but also *what I am*."[10]

We shall not be saved by anything less than commitment,

[8] Gabriel Marcel, *The Mystery of Being*, Pt. II (Chicago: Henry Regnery Co., 1960), p. 77.
[9] Blaise Pascal, *Pensées*, p. 151.
[10] *Op. cit.*, p. 77.

and the commitment will not be effective unless it finds expression in a committed fellowship. If we have any knowledge of human nature, we begin by rejecting the arrogance of self-sufficiency. Committed men need the fellowship not because they are strong, but because they are—and know that they are—fundamentally sinful and weak.

It is generally recognized that though commitment is of the first importance, men may have more than one object of their commitment. The full commitment of millions of Germans, prior to and during the Great War, was to Adolf Hitler and *his* cause. Other millions are today committed to Marxism. This is why it is now recognized that Marxian communism is fundamentally a religion rather than a mere economic or political system. The fact that it denies God does not keep it from being religious. Christians have no monopoly on commitment; they simply have a different object. A Christian is a person who confesses that, amidst the manifold and confusing voices heard in the world, there is one Voice which supremely wins his full assent, uniting all his powers, intellectual and emotional, into a single pattern of self-giving. That Voice is Jesus Christ. A Christian not only believes *that* He was; he believes *in Him* with all his heart and strength and mind. Christ appears to the Christian as the one stable point or fulcrum in all the relativities of history. Once the Christian has made this primary commitment he still has perplexities, but he begins to know the joy of being used for a mighty purpose, by which his little life is dignified.

CHAPTER 2

The Call to Enlistment

He . . . sets us to the tasks which He has to fulfil for our time. He commands.

—Albert Schweitzer

The Church of Jesus Christ is a sleeping giant. Its unrealized potential is almost staggering to contemplate. There exists in people today a vast amount of goodwill; there is genuine desire to be used. This desire has been revealed, in a most dramatic way, by the multitude of volunteers for the United States Peace Corps. The desire is real and the resources are rich, but we have not found the right combination. The harvest is plentiful, and there are potential harvesters, but the effective call has not yet been made. J. H. Oldham stands nearly alone in that he has provided a reappraisal of what the Church might be, in a mood that is at once candid and hopeful. His remark to Paul Tillich states the paradox of faith and frustration. "You know, Tillich," he reports himself as saying, "Christianity has no meaning for me whatsoever apart from the Church, but I sometimes feel as though the Church as it actually exists is the source of all my doubts and difficulties."[1]

While there is a reservoir of goodwill, there is also in-

[1] J. H. Oldham, *Life Is Commitment* (New York: Association Press, 1959), p. 85.

creasing resistance. The resistance to the gospel in America is not dissimilar to that generally observed in Europe some years ago and may be understood as part of a cultural phase. According to the calm appraisal of a number of acute observers, the resistance to *any* Christian message is greater in the sixties of our century than it was in the fifties. This is seen not only in the writings of self-styled intellectuals, but also in the expressed judgments of the rank and file, particularly of the young. We have to understand, then, the paradox of simultaneous goodwill and antagonism if we are to have any clear notion of the scope of the Christian task, the possibility of its achievement, and its probable price in human effort or courage. The perfect text is that of I Corinthians 16:9: "A wide door for effective work has opened to me, and there are many adversaries." This double truth is especially obvious now, when many people refuse to listen long enough to know what is said, and when the forces arrayed against us are truly formidable. We must find ways to make the contemptuous listen, and this will not be easy.

The value of knowing that the situation of the committed Christian is hard—and getting harder each day—cannot be overestimated. When we know this thoroughly we realize that we cannot win or even survive with the attitude of business-as-usual. It is wholly possible that our situation is harder, in some ways, than was that of the early Christians who operated in the dying culture of classical Greece and Rome, for, though we have the advantage of a supposed general acquaintance with the gospel, we have also the enormous disadvantage that millions of people look upon it as the wave of the past. People who feel our spiritual predicament naturally look for something fresh and new, but, for the most part, it does not occur to them that this may be found in a rediscovery of Christ, who is actually far ahead of us so far as the vitality of culture is concerned.

True recovery is never a matter of going backward for the sake of re-establishing an older pattern, but rather of *uncovering* what has been hidden or overlaid and therefore forgotten. The purpose of such uncovering is the potential effect upon the present and the future. We go back to the New Testament, therefore, not as antiquarians and not as mere historians, but in the hope of finding hints of vitality of which our time is relatively unaware. We ought not, for example, to speak of recovering the lost provinces, if this means an attempt to return to the pattern of an earlier day, partly because this is an effort which never succeeds. We should speak, instead, of occupying the lost provinces in new and creative ways and of making spiritual strides which no previous generation has known or even imagined. Commitment is never real unless it leads to mission, and the mission of Christians is always one which points forward. If we are to go forward we must rid our minds of accepted ideas of what a true Church is, or ought to be, much as the research scientists of great industries, when they seek to make radical improvements, find it necessary to free their minds of current conceptions of what manufactured products ought to be like. In some industries, notably in the production of film, radical improvement has resulted from such total reappraisal, which begins by a new hard look at the original experiment.

As we try to follow a good scientific procedure—going back to the original reaction and looking at it afresh as far as possible—we must make a conscious effort to disabuse ourselves of views which are so widely held that they are assumed without argument or even unconsciously. One of these views is that the Church of Jesus Christ is primarily a hierarchy of professionally religious men. That this is assumed to be the truth is shown by the way in which current religious scenes in news photographs are supposed to include, whenever possible, representatives of the various hierarchies.

The religious pages of the newspapers are mostly about clergymen. It cannot be too strongly pointed out that there was *no* Christian hierarchy when Christ gave the Sermon on the Mount and told the little group that they could be the preservative to keep civilization from decay. Our common mistake is to read back into the original what *we* experience. This is why, in medieval paintings, the original apostles tended to look like Italian priests.

Another pattern, against the domination of which we must be eternally on our guard, is that of the Church as the authoritarian repository of truth. When this conception is accepted uncritically it is almost impossible to avoid thinking of the Church as something on the defensive, like a castle being besieged, but being miraculously unhurt and always holding its store of truth unsullied by attacking heresies.[2] There are many reasons why this conception is inadequate, one of them being that a successful holding operation is something which no person can perform. If we are not advancing we are already retreating. Another reason is that no inerrant body of truth exists or can exist, so far as mortal men are concerned. We can be grateful to Paul Tillich for his unrelenting insistence on "The Protestant Principle"— that man's involvement in the finite predicament renders every claim to infallibility suspect. What the Church represents is not a repository of unchanging truth, but an open-ended search for God's will in our lives, both individually and in the redemptive fellowship. Instead of an unchanging certainty of the kind presumed by those whose faith is a collection of infallible proof-texts, finite men have the awesome responsibility of sharing in the possession of the liberating keys. What is laid upon us is neither a peculiar wisdom denied to others nor a doctrine in which we can take pride, but a

[2] Even the passage about the Church and the Gates of Hell (Matthew 16:18) presents the Church as on the offensive. Thus the clear implication of Christ's own words is exactly the opposite of what we tend to assume.

responsibility to share in a difficult task.

There can be no better starting point for a radical reappraisal of the nature of the Church than a sustained effort to
rediscover the secret of the amazing vitality of early Christianity. Every thoughtful person, as he considers the victory
of the early Church against apparently insurmountable odds,
is deeply moved. Once the Church was represented first by a
little band of dejected fishermen going back to the Sea of
Galilee, and later by one hundred twenty people gathered in
a simple upper room in Jerusalem. Even to the eyes of the
neutral but fair observer, Gamaliel, the movement seemed
likely to collapse.[3] It went on from weakness to strength; it
survived; and finally it provided the center of an enduring
civilization when the dominance of Greece and Rome had
come to an end. If we are wise, we shall view this story not
only with reverential gratitude; we shall also—with the eyes
of those who seek a true pattern of the Christian movement
—view it as perhaps applicable to the needs and problems of
our own day.

It is well known that various Christian groups have
claimed to make the standard of their own work and organization nothing more and nothing less than the New
Testament standard. William Penn's famous slogan, "Primitive Christianity Revived," has been the inspiration of various denominations since the phrase was first coined in the
seventeenth century. Sincere as this effort has been, however,
we must recognize the justification of cynical observers who
have noted the great variety of the supposed New Testament
patterns in modern Church life. Some have made the New
Testament Church idea the basis for the necessity of immer-
sion, some for the denial of the requirement of any physical
baptism at all, some for the prohibition of instrumental

---

[3] See Acts 5:33-39. The Jewish leader is remembered for the fact that
he was wise enough to recognize the possibility of enduring success for
the new movement.

music and others for Christian communism. This variety of judgment, and consequent controversy, about the nature of the early Church should be a sufficient warning against supposing that there is any single detailed pattern which can provide a test of ecclesiastical validity. The truth is that the New Testament does not record any single, wholly consistent pattern of the kind usually sought.

Another important consideration, which bears upon the effort to recover the primitive Christian pattern, is that the first way is not necessarily the best. There is no reason why the Christian society might not be able to improve through the centuries. The principle of development, so well supported by John Henry Newman in the days when he was part of the Oxford Movement, is wholly intelligent and intelligible. The Church ought to be able to grow as science or politics can grow. The primitive Church had no popes, but this is no clinching argument against the wisdom of having popes later, providing there is some good reason for having them. In the same manner the early Church owned no buildings, but this does not mean that it was wicked or unchristian for later generations to erect ecclesiastical structures. If anyone says that we ought not to have organs because we have no evidence that early Christians used them, we should, by the same logic, be forced to avoid steam heat, Sunday Schools, Christian colleges, publishing houses, and a thousand other features of contemporary Christian life. We need not go back to the original pattern with superstitious obedience, but we are wise, when we see some central feature of early Christianity which helps to account for its success, to ask whether this can be incorporated into our present practice. What we want is not slavish adherence to a supposedly perfect and changeless pattern, which is in fact nonexistent; rather, we want the humility to re-examine our own conventional expectations and standards in the light of something which succeeded—in sharp contrast to our own mixed record in contemporary life.

One of the most surprising facts about the early Church was its fundamental similarity to a military band. This is hard for us to recognize today because the ordinary successful church of the twentieth century is about as different from an army as anything we can imagine. Instead of being under anything resembling military discipline we pride ourselves on our "freedom." We go and come as we like, as no soldier can do; we give or withhold giving as we like; we serve when we get around to it. Obedience is considered an irrelevant notion, and the theme of "Onward Christian Soldiers" is so alien to our experience that some churches avoid the hymn entirely. A few avoid it on the mistaken assumption that it glorifies killing, which of course it does not. The military metaphor seems strained when it is applied to smartly dressed men and women riding in air-conditioned cars to air-conditioned "churches."

Far from thinking of the Church in military terms, we think of it as a civil society which people join freely and leave freely, though they often seem, oddly enough, to be born into it. It is a society which makes mild claims, even in regard to attendance at its meetings, which appear to be its most important functions. In this regard it is in sharp contrast to the luncheon clubs which have attained great importance in current civilization, partly because they have strict attendance requirements. Clubs normally demand that failure to attend be made up by attendance at other units, but churches are more tolerant on this point. While soldiers are specifically under authority and may, consequently, be sent anywhere without the right of refusal, most people would smile at the idea of the Church sending them on missions which they could not refuse. A slight approximation to the military pattern is exhibited by the Mormons, whose young

men normally donate at least a year of their lives to missionary duty, but the idea has not been generally adopted by other
groups. The notion of enlisting Church members as recruits
sounds very strange to modern ears. This reaction tells us
something significant about the Church of the twentieth
century; it tells us how far we have drifted!

The idea of the Church as a military company was by no
means strange to early Christians. Indeed, military language
can be found in various parts of the New Testament. It need
hardly be said that this language had no reference to killing,
or preparation for destruction, but rather to the mood of
men and women whose responsibilities were of the same
demanding character as those of enlisted persons. Thus it
seems wholly natural to read of "Epaphroditus my brother
and fellow worker and fellow soldier" (Philippians 2:25);
of "a good soldier of Christ Jesus," with his share of suffering (II Timothy 2:3); of "Archippus our fellow soldier"
(Philemon 2); of "the whole armor of God" (Ephesians
6:11). It is perfectly clear that early Christians considered
Christ their Commander-in-Chief, that they were in a company of danger which involved great demands upon their
lives, and that to be a Christian was to be engaged in Christ's
service. It cannot be too emphatically pointed out that such
"service" was not remotely similar to what we call a "service"
today, a polite gathering of auditors, sitting in comfortable
pews listening to a clergyman and a choir.

We do not know as well as we should like to know what
the meetings of the first Christians were like in detail, but
we have in the New Testament some extremely helpful in-
dications. In any case we know enough to realize that these
meetings were not at all what we think of as characteristic
Christian gatherings in our own day. The probability is that
there was no human audience at all and not the slightest
thought of a pattern in which one man is expected to be in-

spired to speak fifty-two times a year, while the rest are never so inspired. A clear indication of procedure is provided by Colossians 3:16 where we read "as you teach and admonish one another in all wisdom." The most reasonable picture which these words suggest is that of a group of modest Christians sitting in a circle in some simple room, sharing with one another their hopes, their failures, and their prayers. The key words are "one another." There are no mere observers or auditors; *all are involved*. Each is in the ministry; each needs the advice of the others; and each has something to say to the others. The picture of mutual admonition seems strange to modern man, but the strangeness is only a measure of *our* essential decline from something of amazing power. The contemporary Communists have taken over the essentials of this pattern for their own dissimilar purposes, but we must remember that they did not invent it. They took it over after Christians had largely abandoned it. Their doing so may constitute a justified rebuke to those who take their Christianity so lightly that they never see themselves as members of a task force.

That early Christians, when they met, expected general participation in vocal expression is the whole point of I Corinthians 14:26-33. Indeed, the expected participation was so nearly universal that rules had to be made to avoid consequent confusion. If there had been the expectation of only one speaker, as in a characteristic contemporary Christian service, it would have been pointless to warn that "you can all prophesy one by one, so that all may learn and all be encouraged" (I Corinthians 14:31). It is obvious that women spoke. Otherwise the Apostle Paul would not have made a rule against it, a rule which he seems later to have abandoned when he wrote Galatians 3:28. Rules are not made to prohibit what no one ever does.

Important as are these evidences which the Epistles provide concerning the character of the early Christian movement, the evidences gleaned from the words and actions of Christ Himself are even more important. Of special significance is Christ's contact with two Roman soldiers whc were centurions. One of these military officers appears neaɪ the beginning of the Gospel, and the other appears near the end. The first centurion, whose confrontation with Christ is recorded in Matthew 8:5-13,[4] asked Christ to heal his servant who was suffering from paralysis. Christ offered to go to the sufferer, but the Roman officer replied quickly that this would not be necessary. He pointed out that he understood about commands and obedience *because* he was a soldier and therefore, like Christ, was *also* under authority. We are told that Jesus "marveled" and gave this Roman the greatest praise which the Gospel records in connection with any historical figure. "Not even in Israel have I found such faith," He said.

This is the sort of account on which we ought to meditate in depth if we are really serious in our effort to understand the nature of the movement which Christ was instituting. There was an obvious kinship of mind between the officer and Christ, a kinship which led to mutual understanding. It seems paradoxical to us that a military officer would understand Christ better than did the apostles, but that is only because we have constructed our own version of what was going on. If we were to realize the fundamentally arduous character of the original Christian movement we should be less surprised at what the story of the centurion reveals. It would seem less paradoxical. We should see the significance of the word "also."

The evidence given by Christ's encounter with the first centurion is corroborated and strengthened by his encounter

[4] And in a slightly different form in Luke 7:1-10. Both Matthew and Luke represent the centurion as using the crucial Greek word *gar*, "also."

with the second, the one who stood by the cross. This man, we are told, "stood facing him" as "Jesus uttered a loud cry, and breathed his last" (Mark 15:39). His duty as a soldier kept him there when most of the disciples were conspicuously absent. The great fact about the occasion is that the scene which the officer saw made him *understand*. As Christ's physical life ebbed away, the soldier was heard to say, "Truly this man was a son of God!" The fact that it was a soldier who had this revelatory reaction is highly significant. He understood that the suffering he observed was really that of a military prisoner from a new kind of army, an army not for destruction but for redemption.

If we realize that Christ was organizing a genuine "company" many points immediately become clear. Herein is the significance of the cryptic "Follow me." He was not advising people to go to church, or even to attend the synagogue; He was, instead, asking for recruits in a company of danger. He was asking not primarily for belief, but for commitment with consequent involvement. It is significant that the first of those who answered this call to enlistment followed Him *before* they knew who He was. The recognition of Christ's true character, in Matthew 16, comes long after the successful appeal of Matthew 4:19. The well-known words are far more understandable if we see them as the call of a recruiting officer, "And he said to them, 'Follow me, and I will make you fishers of men.' Immediately they left their nets and followed him." The fact that the responsive fishermen did not know who He was is what gives such enduring appeal to the words with which Albert Schweitzer concluded his greatest book:

He comes to us as One unknown, without a name, as of old, by the lake-side, He came to those men who knew Him not. He speaks to us the same word: "Follow thou me!" and sets us to the tasks which He has to fulfil for our time. He commands.

And to those who obey Him, whether they be wise or simple, He will reveal Himself in the toils, the conflicts, the sufferings which they shall pass through in His fellowship, and, as an ineffable mystery, they shall learn in their own experience Who He is.[5]

Such recruitment led inevitably to the close fellowship of a *company*. The more genuine the commitment, the more necessary the fellowship of mutual concern and support became. There is no suggestion that the early Christians wore a uniform or had any other external marks of a separate order, but they traveled back and forth between particular companies with a tirelessness that amazes us if we are willing to reflect upon the expenditure of energy which was involved. When one sector was hard pressed, reinforcements were rushed in from another. Thus, in the earliest book of the New Testament, I Thessalonians, we find the Apostle Paul keeping in touch with the little bands quite as though he were a general. In order to check again on the development of the fellowship in Thessalonica, Paul stayed in Athens alone and sent his lieutenant right back to the northern front. "We sent Timothy, our brother and God's servant in the gospel of Christ, to establish you in your faith" (I Thessalonians 3:2). The fact that the demands of the Company of the Committed—such as constant travel under arduous conditions— were accepted without argument and without complaint provides one of our best insights into "the way." It was not a bed of roses, but it was not supposed to be. What else were they to expect, since their Leader had been crucified? It seemed normal for Paul to charge Timothy to "wage the good warfare" (I Timothy 1:18).

Whenever the original pattern of the company has been tried, great results have followed. The two most conspicuous

[5] *The Quest of the Historical Jesus* (New York: The Macmillan Company, 1936), p. 401.

efforts in Christian history have been the organization of the Society of Jesus in the sixteenth century and the organization of the Salvation Army in the nineteenth century. Both experiments have involved failure as well as success, but their total effect has been so remarkable that we neglect them at our peril. Though Ignatius Loyola had no specific design of opposing the Reformation when he wrote his *Spiritual Exercises* and founded his famous Society, it is nevertheless true that the Jesuits were effective in producing a genuine historical change of direction. They were instrumental, through their missionary and educational activities, in saving great sections of northern Europe for the Roman Catholic Church and in regaining lost territory. Loyola's success is in large measure due to the fact that he organized his followers, with hard demands, after the fashion of a military company. His first desire was to use the phrase "The Company of Jesus" because he envisaged a campaign. The key to his entire enterprise is found in his terse reference, "Christ, our Commander-in-Chief." Loyola combined two elements of success which went together perfectly: his own soldierly experience prior to his commitment, and his recognition of the militant character of original Christianity.

The only language Loyola could speak was the language of a warrior; it was always the banner and the battle, obedience and command, company and militia. . . . He demanded the virtues of a soldier but renounced the conditions that fostered them.[6]

An important step in modern history was made in March 1539 when the men who had been influenced by the dream which possessed Loyola met and unanimously decided to remain united and to "organize a new *campagnia* which

[6] Ludwig Marcuse, *Soldier of the Church, A Life of Ignatius Loyola* (London: Methuen & Company, Ltd., 1939), p. 215.

will not end with us." This particular use of words is instructive, for it helps us to remember that the only purpose of a company is a campaign. Many people have written of the early Jesuits, in praise or in condemnation, but all agree that they *made a difference*. Heinrich Boehmer has provided, in his great book on the movement, one of the clearest explanations of Loyola's method:

Finally, as a matter of principle, he avoided obligating himself to any permanent service at a particular place or to any definite form of activity. His one desire was to awaken, evangelize, organize, assist, *everywhere;* but never bind himself to any one thing or place permanently. He even retired from the direction of the new institutions which he had founded as soon as he was completely assured of their continuance.[7]

The fact that Loyola's movement is not adequate for the needs of our own day should not blind us to its fundamental strength. It is inadequate because it is fundamentally denominational in purpose, being concerned with the militant recovery of *one church* rather than the *whole Church of Christ;* it is limited to those who have some degree of separation from the common life of marriage and secular work. But those limitations are not intrinsic to the idea of a company enlisted in Christ's cause. What we must form, unless we are to go into decay, is a company which includes representatives of all denominations, which understands fully that in Christ there is neither male nor female, which expects commitment to Christ *in* common life rather than in separation from it, and which is infused with the sense of urgency possessed by those who are fully involved in a campaign. The strategy of renewal lies not in organizing a *militia Christi* within the Church, but in recasting the entire conception of the Church in the light of Christ's call to enlist-

[7] Heinrich Boehmer, *The Jesuits, An Historical Study* (Philadelphia: The Castle Press, 1928), p. 73.

ment. The Church so remade will be as different from the conventional organization with which we are now familiar as Christ's band of the crusading Seventy was different from the synagogue of the first century A.D.

In leaving the synagogue and concentrating upon the explosive band, Christ was not renouncing the fellowship of the devout but was, instead, giving it a new and virile character. Emphatically, we must note that He was not rejecting the synagogue or meetinghouse version of religion in favor of mere individual commitment. Instead, He was making the social character of this commitment far more obvious and demanding. The early Christians did not seek God's will in individual isolation. Instead, they found a fellowship so intense that it was of a wholly different character from that of people who happen to sit in the same room listening to a homily. Instead of being an audience they were actors! This is why, though the word "synagogue" had come to refer to a building, the word "Church," for the early Christians, could not possibly have done so.

We cannot understand the idea of a company apart from the concept of *involvement*. What we seek is not a fellowship of the righteous or of the self-righteous, but rather a fellowship of men and women who, though they recognize that they are inadequate, nevertheless can be personally involved in the effort to make Christ's kingdom prevail. Perhaps the greatest single weakness of the contemporary Christian Church is that millions of supposed members are not really involved at all and, what is worse, do not think it strange that they are not. As soon as we recognize Christ's intention to make His Church a militant company we understand at once that the conventional arrangement cannot suffice. There is no real chance of victory in a campaign if ninety per cent of the soldiers are untrained and uninvolved, but that is exactly where we stand now. Most alleged

Christians do not now understand that loyalty to Christ means sharing personally in His ministry, going or staying as the situation requires.

The churches which are succeeding best are those in which the involvement of the rank and file of the members is most nearly complete. This means a general acceptance, on the part of the total membership, of the responsibility of being official representatives of Jesus Christ in daily life. It means a fundamental denial of that kind of division of labor in which the majority have a secular responsibility and a minority have a Christian responsibility. There is always some need of a division of labor in life, partly because people have radically different gifts, but a division of labor is damaging and vicious when it leaves the promotion of the gospel to a few, while the others merely support them in such work. The easiest way to undermine Christian responsibility in a college, for instance, is to appoint one man chaplain, if the consequent understanding is that the other professors, in the supposedly secular departments, are thus set free from real responsibility for the Christian cause on the campus.

It is strange to see how slow we are to understand what the acceptance of the idea of a Christian company entails. Thus, when we organize a commitment service, we tend, unless we make a conscious effort at involvement, to have the familiar pattern of the single performer. If, by contrast, many share in the observance—whether in reading Scripture or in public prayer or in admonition—there are two enormous gains. One is that even those who do not participate vocally begin to have a sense that they are more than audience; the other is that the commitment of those who do participate vocally is normally made deeper and more genuine. Preaching may not, in some instances, be helpful to those who listen, but it is almost always helpful to those who speak. This is partly because expression deepens impression and partly because the speaker immediately achieves a public identification with the cause, from which he is consequently less likely to turn back. Since commitment is strengthened by public involvement, the more involvement the better. Therefore the Christian ideal must always be the complete elimination of the concept of the laity in favor of the exciting concept of the universal ministry.

If we are to take seriously the transformation of the Church as we know it into a genuine order, we must voluntarily accept an agreed discipline. Once a Christian has become a member of Christ's company he must be ready to give up some of his personal freedom, much as any soldier—and even as any Communist—does. He may, for example, no longer be the sole arbiter of his own time and energy; and he cannot be free to use all of his money on his own self-indulgence. He may have to give up his own personal plans in order to engage in a contemporary equivalent of Timothy's hurried return to Thessalonica. He is almost certain to give up some connections with clubs and societies which, though they may be innocent or valuable in their aims, are far too numerous in most modern lives. There will always be a sense in which a person who takes seriously his commitment to Christ will have to learn to travel light, giving up some particular involvements in order to make other involvements more truly revolutionary.

One of the areas of experience in which the acceptance of discipline is most important for modern man is that of the right use of time. Our relation to time is highly paradoxical in that, though we live in an age marked by time-saving devices, we seem to be ever more hectic in running from appointment to appointment. Because we do not have to use precious time, as all of our ancestors did, in carrying water, grinding flour, and weaving cloth, we should, theoretically, have more free time available, but we do not. The trouble seems to be that we presume on the advantage of our inventions by deliberately adding to the number of our engagements until our lives are fragmented. Too many commitments amount virtually to none. The only commitment which is significant is that which has about it a certain singularity or even priority.

Acceptance of discipline is the price of freedom. The pole vaulter is not free to go over the high bar except as he disciplines himself rigorously day after day. The freedom of the surgeon to use his drill to cut away the bony structure, close to a tiny nerve without severing it, arises from a similar discipline. It is doubtful if excellence in any field comes in any other way. John Milton was revealing something of his own creative power when he wrote, "There is not that thing in the world of more grave and urgent importance, throughout the whole life of man, than is discipline."

One of the best secrets of the discipline of time is the fuller date book. This seems, at first, like a gratuitous paradox but appears, upon reflection, to be most reasonable. If a man will go through his date book and fill in empty places with really important commitments, including those to meditation, to solitude, to prayer, and to writing, his temptations to scatter his energies will be more ably resisted. The temptation to waste an evening in shallow talk or in watching a succession of television westerns can be better handled if a decision has already been made to read a great book or to engage in the arduous task of recording one's reflections. In the same way, much of the problem of time can be met by including, in the year's program, engagements with one's family and friends—for they deserve attention also. Thus, the prior engagement, whatever its character, is a practical way of avoiding the constant necessity of making little decisions at the moment and thereby it achieves liberation.

Of course, no decent person will be so hard with himself, or others, that a planned use of time will be inflexible. It is obvious that in any life real emergencies may arise, and we must, consequently, be ready to change our plans when there is a sufficient reason for doing so. There is a third way, better than either the inflexibility of a machine or the emptiness of the unexamined life. Dr. Samuel Johnson, after referring admiringly to the methodical life of John Milton, without which the blind man would certainly never have produced *Paradise Lost,* went on to say, "He that lives in the world will sometimes have the succession of his practice broken and confused."[8] This we know and this we need to know, but a man cannot even change his plan unless he has one. Certainly one cannot be in the Company of the Committed unless he has a rule by which he tries to live. It is a great mistake to suppose, as some do, that the acceptance of such a discipline, as an alternative to empty freedom, will make Christians into overmeticulous and self-righteous Pharisees. This may have been the danger once, but it is certainly not the primary danger now. The primary danger now is that of those who, in Eliot's strong phrase, suppose that they are emancipated because they are merely "unbuttoned."

The discipline we need is not something which we can learn alone. We become trained and disciplined for service only as we are yoked together. Thus, significantly, it is in Christ's clearest call to personal commitment—that in which He says, "Come to me"—that He also says, "Take my yoke upon you." The Company of Christ is tied together by Christ's yoke. That is why "yokefellow" is a synonym for committed Christian.[9] Though the younger generation does

---

[8] Samuel Johnson, *Lives of the Poets,* essay on Milton.
[9] See Matthew 11:29 and Philippians 4:3.

not understand it now, every farm child of the early part of our century understood very well that no colt is normally trained alone. It is "hitched" with one already well trained. Herein lies the powerful significance of the idea that only the meek—i.e., the disciplined—will ever occupy the land.[10] Gerald Heard has rendered good service in explaining meekness in a way that is very different from the popular one. For what, he asks, did the Greeks use the word *praos?*

They used it for wild animals which had been tamed, trained, for wild horses which had been made able to work with men. There is then in this definition, nothing weak or spiritless but rather the description of an energy which, instead of exploding, is now channelled and directed. The tamed are not the tame. . . . The trained are those whose powerful impulses have been put into understanding service.[11]

One rare but powerful item of discipline is the requirement that the recruit of the company undertake a personal experience of solitude at least once a month. This is patterned consciously on the experience of Christ who periodically went alone, even at the price of temporary separation from the needs of His fellows. The justification of aloneness is not that of refined self-indulgence, but rather a consequent enrichment of one's subsequent contribution. A person who is always available is not worth enough when he *is* available. Everyone engaged in public life will realize the extreme difficulty of getting away each month for a period of five or six hours, but the difficulty is not a good reason for rejecting the discipline. It is the men and women who find it hardest to get away who need the redemptive solitude most sorely. They need to be where they are free

[10] See Psalm 37:11 and Matthew 5:5.
[11] Gerald Heard, *The Code of Christ* (New York: Harper & Brothers, 1941), pp. 63-64; see also Heard's Appendix, "On the Use of the Word *Praos*," pp. 169 ff.

from the compulsion of chit-chat, from the slavery of the telephone, and even from the newspaper. A Christianity which understands itself will make ample provision for retreat houses in which such solitude is expected and protected.

At the very time when we are beginning to realize how formidable are the forces arrayed against Christianity in the modern world, an old yet new conception of the fellowship of those enlisted in Christ's cause is re-emerging. This may be one of the times when the greatness of the need may be matched by the vitality of the response. There is no real hope of such vitality unless and until we understand what Christian enlistment means. Because the trouble we face is more serious than we ordinarily suppose, the solution of our problems will likewise lie along deeper lines than those to which we are accustomed.

CHAPTER 3

The Vocation of Witness

I am obliged to bear witness because I hold, as it were, a particle of light, and to keep it to myself would be equivalent to extinguishing it.

—Gabriel Marcel

We know something important about the Christian Church when we know that it is clearly intended to be a company. Such an understanding helps mightily in the recovery of the mood of urgency. The true inwardness of the Church is reflected, not in the Temple, which Christ said could be destroyed without loss, and not in the synagogue, which He seems to have abandoned with deliberate decision, but in the sending out of the Seventy. The Church is intended as a concrete answer to the prayer that laborers be sent forth to the harvest. The Company of Jesus is not people streaming to a shrine; and it is not people making up an audience for a speaker; it is laborers engaged in the harvesting task of reaching their perplexed and seeking brethren with something so vital that, if it is received, it will change their lives.

Once we have this understanding of what the general nature of the Church is, we need to be more specific in examining the concrete tasks to which the gathered workers are assigned. What are the members of the company supposed to do? To this Christ gives an answer which is truly

45

shocking to modern man. He says that their first task is to give testimony. This is shocking to our generation because it goes directly against the grain of our most cherished ideas. Perhaps in our childhood some of us heard men and women rise in a prayer meeting to tell what the Lord had done for them. Or perhaps we went to one of the midweek sessions at a Christian Science church and heard person after person rise to tell of long illness or defeat succeeded by experiences of health and victory. We likely said that this might have been valuable to another generation but that it was not valuable to ours, and we, accordingly, vowed never to engage in such exhibitions.

This negative reaction of an entire generation is wholly understandable. As a matter of fact, many of the testimonies tended to become mere stereotypes, the same expressions appearing with repetitious and boring regularity. Furthermore, there was always the danger of ostentation and spiritual boasting. Many people decided that while they might continue as believers in Christ, they would never be caught dead telling anyone else about it. They determined to be discreet and quiet about their faith, to let their lives speak, if any speaking was required, and to avoid, at all costs, forcing their opinions upon anyone else. They did not want to emulate the people who invaded the privacy of others, because, they said, they did not want to have their own privacy invaded. Thus, the time came when the rejection of testimony seemed to be supported by highly moral reasons, including modesty, sincerity, and respect for others. Above all, the motive seemed to be the rejection of display of personal virtue.

However understandable this revulsion from testimony on the part of an entire generation may have been, it runs directly counter to the teaching of our Commander-in-chief. Indeed, Christ's first command to the little group gathered on the mountain is so alien to our popular mood that some readers miss it entirely. But the truth is that, according to Matthew's account, Christ's first word of command to the group was the injunction to engage in *witness*. After He had made the incredible prediction that their fellowship could be the salt which would preserve the world from decay, He proceeded to say that they were also the light of the world and from this observation came the direct command, "Let your light . . . shine" (Matthew 5:16). They were told that the light that was in them dare not be covered or hidden, that it must be lifted up for all men to see; in short, they were admonished to make a visible witness. And then, as though to counter in advance the expected objection of modern man concerning the danger of personal display, He said that the purpose, far from being their self-glorification, was to give glory to God.

As the contemporary Christian faces this clear injunction, he is bound to re-examine his own prejudices. Perhaps he has been wrong in his complete rejection of the theology of witness. If, believing in the Lordship of Christ, we find our views at variance with the bulk of His teaching, we are always bound to engage in re-examination of our own views. At this point we find that Christ's insistence upon the priority of witness receives corroboration from a surprising source, modern secular philosophy. A striking example is found in the work of the French existentialist, Gabriel Marcel, particularly in his Gifford Lectures at the University of Aberdeen and in *The Philosophy of Existence*.[1] His "Testimony and Existentialism" is one of the great philosophical essays of modern times. The philosopher wrote the essay, he tells us, not so much to define existentialism "as to throw some light on what seems to me its essence by

---

[1] Gabriel Marcel. *The Philosophy of Existence* (London: Harvill Press, 1948), p. 67.

bringing out its key notions." Consequently, the essay is one of the best introductions to existentialism as a movement of thought.

Marcel approaches the subject of testimony by examining what occurs in a court of law, which, of course, cannot be conducted without the introduction of testimony. In a trial we want to know what the objective truth is, but there is no conceivable way of finding this out except as we pay attention to persons who claim to have had particular historical experiences which bear directly upon the question being examined. Truth in the abstract or in detachment from human experience may conceivably exist, but it is never known to us. Each one who is brought to the witness stand is brought for only one reason, the supposition that some bit of *evidence* is included in His life experience. Marcel is particularly helpful in his analysis of the moral responsibility of the person who has some evidence which relates to what is at hand. In the first place, he is not free to withhold it; in the second place, the giving of the witness is a solemn undertaking in which the individual who witnesses binds himself under oath. Once he takes oath he is entirely committed; he cannot withdraw; he is involved; he cannot, accordingly, retract without complete loss of integrity. Unless you stake everything on what you say you cannot be a witness.[2]

If a man is being tried for murder and I happen to possess, in my little stream of experience, the evidence that the accused man was actually at a different spot at the time of his alleged murderous act, I am not free to withhold it. If I do withhold it I am myself a murderer, for I destroy an innocent man by my silence. The failure to witness in such a situation is a highly immoral act. Thus it is clear that we

[2] It is perhaps obvious that the involvement is equally great if a person elects, as American practice permits, to engage in affirmation rather than in oath.

do not avoid the moral ambiguities of testimony by mere refusal to testify. The dangers of the old-fashioned testimony meeting, which the members of our generation have seen so clearly, are real, but it is possible that the dangers of our alternative way of life, the rejection of testimony, may be equally real and ultimately more damaging.

The importance of all this for the Christian company is immense. The recruits of the company are precisely those who are called to be witnesses to their relation to one another and to their Lord. It is not that the Church is formed first and then, subsequently, is expected to witness. Rather, the original fellowship is the fellowship of witness; this is what it is formed to accomplish. "Conversion," says Marcel in a memorable sentence, "is the act by which man is called to be a witness."[3] The call to witness is a call which men can answer affirmatively or negatively, but one who answers it negatively, however kind and pious he may be, is not in the Company of Jesus. "Since the world of testimony is also that of freedom, it is one in which one can refuse to testify, or else in which one can be a false witness, etc., that is, a world in which there can be sin."[4]

It cannot be too strongly emphasized that all witness necessarily involves the use of the first person singular. My testimony bears, I believe, on something independent of me, something objectively real, but I cannot escape the necessity of my personal affirmation. It is never somebody in general who bears witness; it is always an individual with an individual consciousness. "Some person" is a highly generalized expression, perfectly suitable in abstract discussions, but far removed from the only concrete reality which we know. In the long run I cannot possibly speak for another. All that I can do is to say humbly, yet courageously, "I was there; it

[3] *The Mystery of Being*, Pt. II, p. 133.
[4] *Ibid.*, p. 132.

happened to me; I experienced such and such at such a point in historical time." To be meaningful, testimony must be both personal and historical.

Though it is widely supposed that natural science shows us a realm in which we are free from personal involvement, this conclusion is manifestly false. We use the intricate machines which we have made, but at the end of every scientific road is a person, the individual scientist, who affirms that he has observed. The machine facilitates the sharpness of observation, but cannot avoid its necessity. What we call natural science is possible as a reliable discipline because a number of people, with adequate and relevant preparation of their powers of observation, often succeed in corroborating the witness of one another. Astronomy becomes a science when a fellowship of careful and honorable searchers "see" what another of their number has "seen." The success of the science depends upon the cumulative agreement of the personal testimonies.

When we begin to apply this analysis to religious experience the similarity of pattern is obvious at once. The ultimate thing which anyone can say about the Living God is "I have encountered Him: He has reached me; He stood at my door and knocked, and, when I opened the door, He came in and communed with me." The person who provides such a witness could be wrong; he could be lying; but his is the ultimate evidence. We can, by careful reasoning, provide systematic support for what he reports, or we may undermine it by introducing what seem to be relevant negative considerations, but his evidence is the basic stuff of our entire enterprise. This is the point of Pascal's well-known distinction between the God of philosophers, on the one hand, and the God of Abraham, Isaac, and Jacob, on the other. The God of the philosopher can never be a substitute for the God of faith and experience. In short, philosophy may perform a useful service in *discussing* the testimony, but it is not itself the testimony.

In the long run the only answer to unfaith is the witness of those whose lives are of such a character that their witness is listened to by honest men and women. Millions of people, as in Christ's time, are "harassed and helpless, like sheep without a shepherd" (Matthew 9:36), and they are really waiting to hear someone say, both humbly and bravely, "This I have learned. Here I stand." It is slightly shocking to some modern men and women to realize that when Christ said the laborers were few, He and those to whom He spoke were surrounded by large numbers of priests and semi-professional religious men. The priests in Jerusalem were so numerous that they had to take turns in performing Temple ceremonies. The dearth was of persons who could give the only kind of witness that counts with those looking for help, the kind that is couched in the first person singular. The great need is for men who can say with the man who had been blind, "One thing I know" (John 9:25).

Because modern man will not listen to mere speculation but may listen to the record of experience, whether in science or religion, we may confidently assert that the theology which stresses the trustworthiness and importance of religious experience is likely to return to general favor. Increasingly, the best theology moves from the impersonal to the personal, and, even more importantly, from the third person to the second, so far as the Living God is concerned. The only God worth discussing is the "Absolute Thou," the One to whom men can pray, the One who can meet us on the way in the breaking of bread, in the recognition of our need for penitence, and in the labor of remaking some little sector of God's world. It will not be surprising if, in our troubled time, we return again and again to Marcel's memorable phrase, "a theology which is not based on testimony must be looked at with suspicion."[5] The brilliant contemporary writer, Edith Hamilton, showed a real sensitivity to the modern mood when she used, as the title of her life of Christ (which includes a chapter on the life of Socrates), *Witness to the Truth*. Whittaker Chambers sensed the same potential response when he called his account of his own life story *Witness*.

Part of the paradox of our time lies in the double fact that we are now ready to listen to witness but are hesitant to give it. We avoid the witness stand insofar as our religion is concerned, with the odd result that although religion is popular its dominant mood is apologetic. Christian colleges want, in many areas, to hide the basic Christian commitment of their institutions, for it is something of which they are slightly ashamed. Many persons are terribly fearful of seeming pious. Something must have occurred in their childhood for them to develop what is essentially a phobia on this point. The strangest result of this phobia is that great numbers of people continue to fight against a danger which may once have been real, but is so no longer. A little realism in observation would teach us that the genuine danger *we* face, whatever our ancestors may have faced, is that of a mood in which people are so terribly apologetic that they refuse to witness at all. A part of wisdom about life is willingness to fight on contemporary rather than on outworn fronts.

The apologetic mood, which resists the making of personal testimony on the grounds of modesty, is surprisingly inconsistent. People defend their failure to testify by reference to their tenderness toward others, but it is easy to observe that such gentility does not extend to other areas of experience. It certainly does not extend to economics and to politics, where we express our opinions endlessly and force-

[5] *Ibid.*, p. 139.

fully. We are not reticent in saying which athletic teams we support and in announcing our support vociferously. How odd that it is only in regard to the spiritual life that we are reticent! It is hard to avoid the conclusion that what poses as a virtue is really a vice. A little self-analysis reveals the fact that what we call humility is actually fear of involvement which is costly in time, in money, and in peace of mind. We avoid witnessing because we recognize that it comes at a high price!

It is one thing to recognize that there is no vital Christianity without witness; it is another to know how a valid witness is to be made. Few are superficial enough to suppose that it can be made effectively by standing up in a crowded room to declare one's allegiance to the cause of Jesus Christ. But if not that way, then how? We can begin our answer by observing that testimony must be in both deed and word. The spoken word is never really effective unless it is backed up by a life, but it is also true that the living deed is never adequate without the support which the spoken word can provide. This is because no life is ever good enough. The person who says naïvely, "I don't need to preach; I just let my life speak," is insufferably self-righteous. What one among us is so good that he can let his life speak and leave it at that? We should make our lives as good as we possibly can, but at the end of the day we are still imperfect and unworthy. If our expressed faith were not better than our practice, we should make practically no progress at all. Anyone can end hypocrisy simply by lowering his principles to accord with his practice, but it is easy to see that the result would be loss rather than gain.

The more we think of it the more we are shocked intellectually by the modish supposition that verbal witness is somehow evil or presumptuous. Such an idea is always the result of shallow thinking which comes as a reaction to a supposed evil of the past, but fails to realize that the alternative to one evil may be another. There has to be a verbal witness because there cannot be communication of important *convictions* without language. "I cannot by being good," says Samuel M. Shoemaker, "tell of Jesus' atoning death and resurrection, nor of my faith in His divinity. The emphasis is too much on me, and too little on Him."[6] We must use words because our faith must be in something vastly greater than ourselves. We make a witness by telling not *who* we are but *whose* we are. Though it would be ridiculous for me to try to make a witness by telling of my own righteousness, which, after all, does not exist, it is not at all ridiculous for me to confess, with candor, to Whom I am committed. This is why the Vocation of Witness belongs necessarily to the Company of the Committed, rather than to the company of the good or the wise or the prudent. The truth is that our words, which can express something of our ultimate loyalty, can be far better than we are, yet for them we are responsible. This seems to be the point of Christ's statement, which is so shocking to our generation, "By your words you will be justified, and by your words you will be condemned" (Matthew 12:37).

The purpose of witness in the law court is justice, but the purpose of witness in the life of the Church is evangelism. By evangelism is meant the deliberate effort to extend the area of Christ's influence, both in individual lives in which this influence is needed and in all areas of common life. The widespread aversion to evangelism seems to rest largely on our difficulty in distinguishing between it and proselytizing. Evangelism is the effort to facilitate the growth of new life, while proselytizing is the effort to enhance the power, prestige, or numbers of one's own particular sect or organization. It ought to be obvious that we can reject the latter while

[6] Samuel M. Shoemaker, *Creating Christian Cells*, Faith at Work, p. 51.

espousing the former, for the former is implicit in any genuine conviction. No one whose life has been truly touched by the life of Christ is free to leave the matter there; he must, as a consequence, extend the boon. We can use many figures to make this clear. One way of clarification is to point out that we dare not let the chain reaction stop with us. No one to whom the love of Christ has been mediated so that he is in some sense a new person, is free to let this stop so long as he lives. If he has been, in any sense, liberated, he must join in the eternal fellowship of liberation. If the enkindling fire (Luke 12:49) which Christ said He came to light has in any sense entered his soul, he cannot rest until he lights as many other fires as possible. In short, a person cannot be a Christian and avoid being an evangelist. Evangelism is not a professionalized job of a few gifted or trained men but is, instead, the unrelenting responsibility of every person who belongs, even in the most modest way, to the Company of Jesus.

The method of evangelism is inevitably the method of testimony. Each man has only one story that is worth telling. This is why the first book of a novelist is often fundamentally autobiographical and also why it is often his best. The best way to reach another life is by saying, as simply as possible, "Whereas I was blind, now I see." This, of course, is the justification for the great Christian journals, like those of John Wesley or John Woolman in the eighteenth century. Each is saying, in the context of his own life, "I have known, at first hand, His healing power." The cynic may ridicule, but the saint merely repeats his story, and often his story receives remarkable corroboration by the stories of others in similar circumstances.

The value of the individual story of Christ's healing power lies largely in the undeniable fact that each human life stands at a unique point in the total web of human experience, and, as a consequence, each one has an approach to others which is not identical with the opportunity of any other human being. If I do not open the door for another, it may never be opened, for it is possible that I may be the only one who holds this particular key. The worker on the production line may have an entree to the life of his fellow worker on the line which can never be matched by any pastor or teacher or professional evangelist. The responsibility of each individual Christian is to do that which no other person can do as well as he can.

While we must never minimize the value of the witness of the separated individual, we should also recognize that sometimes the best witness is that of the Church as a whole. If the Church is primarily a witnessing society, we must try to think how the joint testimony can be made. What can the group do in this regard which the lone individual cannot do? It can build a building, it can raise a spire for men and women to see as a reminder, it can hold meetings which are open to all seekers. Even the very attendance at these meetings, which seems so inadequate, may constitute a witness of a sort. Perhaps it is the only thing that very timid people can do. If so, we must never even give the suggestion of despising it. We can paraphrase Milton by saying that they also serve who only attend. Sometimes they do it with such faithfulness that others take note and follow, perhaps after years of seeming failure to be impressed.

It is in the general setting of the necessity of giving witness and the consequent fellowship of witness that the famous doctrine of the universal priesthood of all believers begins to come alive. All Christians must be in the ministry, whatever their occupations, because the nonwitnessing follower of Christ is a contradiction in terms. If we take seriously Christ's first group order, the command to let our light shine, we dare not let the witness be limited to a small group of the professionally religious. Therefore the ministry of Christ must be universal. It must be universal in three specific ways. It must involve *all places;* it must involve *all times;* it must involve *all Christian persons,* male and female, lay and clerical, old and young.

There is no possibility of a genuine renewal of the life of the Church in our time unless the principle of universal witness is accepted without reservation. The struggle against apathy is so great a task that if we are to achieve even a semblance of a victory we cannot be satisfied to leave Christian work to ordained clergymen. The number one Christian task of our time is the enlargement and adequate training of our ministry which, in principle, includes our total membership. This is a large order, and one which often seems discouraging in prospect, but we cannot settle for anything less and yet be loyal to the idea of Christ's revolutionary company.

It must be admitted that we are now a great distance— not only in practice but even in theory—from the fellowship of universal witness. Millions are merely back-seat Christians, willing to be observers of a performance which the professionals put on, ready to criticize or to applaud, but not willing even to consider the possibility of real participation. Here is the fundamental weakness of the contemporary Church. Millions claim to have some sort of connection with the Church, but it is not a connection of *involvement.* The result is bound to be superficiality. Whatever the nature of the situation, only the involved ever really know anything thoroughly.

Curiously, it is in the most respectable denominations that involvement is most conspicuously absent. Groups such as Jehovah's Witnesses may espouse a confused and irrational theology, but they put the more respected Christian groups to shame by the quality of their participation in the total Christian enterprise. It is not always noted that the very name Jehovah's Witnesses is intended to stress the intrinsic character of the demand for universal testimony. Every member must find his way of participation in personal evangelism from the first day of his association. The shame of those who believe that they have a better theology is that they have not equaled such groups in participation and in courageous witness. Some of the groups which do not seem to us fully Christian in their theological positions are wonderfully Christian in their courage in the face of ridicule and in their willingness to be involved. Perhaps some of them enter the kingdom ahead of the wise and prudent. What is strange is that we seem so unable to distinguish between the intellectual confusion, which we ought to reject, and the admirable involvement, which we ought to emulate.

Even the language of the Jehovah's Witnesses is something to admire, showing remarkable insight. Marcus Bach says,

Local Witnesses constitute not a congregation, but a "company." The place of meeting is not a church; it is a "Kingdom Hall." Leaders of the work may be called ministers—since they are ordained of God—but it is more correct to class them simply as Witnesses. Every Witness is a publisher, for he can become a Witness only by making a covenant with God to "publish" the truth from house to house. Every publisher is expected to devote at least sixty hours a month to the work.[7]

The terms which Marcus Bach has stressed are terms which have been applicable to a great variety of movements in their periods of genuine vitality. It is really more than a coincidence, for example, that one of the earliest names which seventeenth-century Quakers applied to themselves was

[7] Marcus Bach, *They Have Found a Faith* (Indianapolis: Bobbs-Merrill Company, Inc., 1946), p. 37.

"First Publishers of Truth." We smile today, because the terminology is naïve and slightly arrogant, but it went along with a power which their contemporary successors cannot even begin to match. These people of three hundred years ago, who suffered terribly from persecution and faced almost constant ridicule, as Jehovah's Witnesses do today, understood perfectly that a faith which a person is not trying to share is not genuine.

In the conventional pattern of recent generations it has often been assumed that witness is the vocation of the few rather than the many. These few are professional clergymen, individuals ordained in a particular fashion so that they are expected to make a continual witness to the gospel. The deep harm of such a specialized ministry—so different from anything which existed in the beginning of Christianity— has consisted not in the witness which clergymen have made, but in the freedom from witness which others have felt as a consequence of the very existence of the clergy. People have frequently said in essence that they don't have to work at evangelism because they have hired other men to do it. Donating some money in support of the professional seems to liberate the amateur from a sense of responsibility. One of the most damaging assumptions in regard to the Christian movement has been that involved in the distinction between "full-time" Christian witness and ordinary Christian witness. "Full-time" was supposed to distinguish the vocation of the clergy, but patently it does not. The Christian groceryman must give full time, just as the clergyman does —his major time being given in his store. To say that he gives a third of his time to the lay ministry is to accept the very distinction we are pledged to avoid.

It must be admitted that a few clergymen glory in the contrast between their status and that of ordinary Christians. They accept obeisance as a natural right; they monopolize public praying; they learn how to keep themselves in the limelight. There is something about the pastoral office which makes the temptation to egocentricity especially powerful. This is partly because the successful preacher is regularly praised to his face. His mood seems a far cry from that of Christ when He girded Himself with a towel and washed the feet of His followers. Of course, there is a little *pro forma* foot washing today, but it becomes a mere ceremony, and it loses its virtue by being reported in the press. Because some pastors love the limelight and prestige, which is in such contrast to the very meaning of servant or minister, they fear the emergence of the lay ministry. Some pastors see gifted lay leaders as threats to their own eminence. Sometimes they have a sense of danger of the lay ministry comparable to the sense of danger which physicians feel in the distribution of home books of medicine. The pastor sometimes has some justification for his fears when lay leaders emerge without any theological education and consequently with no recognition of the heresy in their own pet opinions.

Our task now is to try to see the entire problem of the ministry in adequate perspective. We may agree that a professionalized ministry is necessary but not sufficient. The chief reason that it is not sufficient is that the job to be done is too big to be accomplished by the work of a minority, no matter how gifted and trained that minority may be. Another reason for the insufficiency of the professionalized ministry is, frankly, that the theological seminaries are not getting the ablest men. In some of our universities the contrast between the divinity students, on the one hand, and the students in law and medicine, on the other hand, is shocking. If we are to have the help of the very ablest persons in the total ministry of Christ, many of them will have to be found in occupations which we term secular. We are not so rich in Christian human resources that we can afford to neglect any. The need is so great that we require all of the help that we can get, and our greatest unexploited resource is the lay membership.

Almost all astute observers agree that the growth of the lay or universal ministry is the growing edge of vital Christianity today. The fact that thousands of men and women who are employed in secular occupations now affirm openly and without undue self-consciousness that they are ministers of Christ in common life is a source of tremendous hope. For many it is absolutely new, and for all who experience it the enrollment in the universal ministry is a powerful stimulus. It is the chief form in which the miracle of involvement now occurs, so far as the Christian faith is concerned. It is the great new Christian fact of our time.

Important as the lay or universal ministry is, it is beset with dangers. The chief danger is that we accept it—though gladly—in such a mild form that our acceptance is almost as harmful as rejection would be. What is meant, all too often, when men speak of the lay ministry, is that members are supposed to give support to the Church as it is. Sometimes it means little more than working on existing committees, giving money, being loyal in attendance at public meetings, and speaking up for the Church when the occasion for defense arises. The trouble with this idea of the function of the laity is that it does not appeal at all to the more adventuresome people whom we so sorely need. This is what J. H. Oldham means when he writes that, though there is now a great deal of talk about the importance of the laity, "the question is approached almost invariably from the wrong end."[8]

Another idea of the lay ministry which is too mild is the notion that lay members are supposed to help the pastor

[8] *Life Is Commitment*, p. 97.

with chores around the church buildings. The idea is that the pastor has a program, a ministry to perform, and ordinary members can be of assistance in the promotion of this work. They are volunteer, unpaid helpers, and thus take the places of paid assistants. But if this is all that we mean by the universal ministry it will never provide the explosive power which our civilization so greatly needs. What we require is not the perpetuation of the current system, but a genuinely new impetus.

The only kind of lay ministry which is worth encouraging is that which makes a radical difference in the entire Christian enterprise. To be truly effective it must erase any difference in kind between the lay and the clerical Christian. The way to erase the distinction, which is almost wholly harmful, is not by the exclusion of professionals from the ministry, as anticlerical movements have tended to do, but rather by the *inclusion* of all in the ministry. The expanded dictum is that in the ministry of Christ there is neither Jew nor Greek, neither bond nor free, neither male nor female, *neither layman nor cleric,* but all are one in Christ Jesus.

At this point in Christian strategy nearly everyone who now considers the matter at all approves the lay ministry, being unable to reject it and also accept the New Testament, but undermines it by a trivial conception of what it means. Accordingly, the burning question now is not whether we believe in the ministry of all Christians, but what we include in that concept. The idea has no real life unless it involves the acceptance of a new kind of leadership, which appears especially in the professions.[9] If Christianity is to be under-

[9] A striking example of the new conception was shown in a recent Layman's Festival which sought to influence the entire life of the capital city of Texas. The leaders were Tom Reavely, a lawyer, and L. D. Haskew, a professor and vice chancellor of the University of Texas. The major speaking was done by Howard Butt, a businessman of Corpus Christi. One of the meetings was with the bar association.

stood not as a retreat from life in the world but as an effort
to transfigure life itself, it follows that the Church needs
the service of men and women at the point where they are
most exposed to the problems of our political and economic
order. "It is through its lay members," says Oldham, "that
the Church makes contact with the life of the world."[10]

The older idea was that the lay members were the pastor's
helpers, but the new and vital idea is that the pastor is the
helper of the ordinary lay members in the performance of
their daily ministry in the midst of secular life. And always,
the problem with which the members need the help of wise
and compassionate pastors or teachers is that of how daily
witness is to be made. Insofar as we really understand the
strategy of the Christian revolution, we shall train our
pastors for this highly specialized and imaginative task. It
cannot be pointed out too clearly, therefore, that emphasis
on the vocation of universal Christian witness, far from
lowering the vision of the function of the pastorate, im-
mensely heightens it. Concern for the universal ministry,
instead of making a specialized and highly trained ministry
unnecessary, makes it all the more significant.

The universal ministry is a great idea, one of the major
ideas of the New Testament, but the hard truth is that it
does not come to flower except as it is nourished deliberately.
Indeed the paradox is that the nourishment of the lay or
universal ministry is the *chief reason* for the development
of a special or partially separated and professionalized ministry. We cannot have an effective universal ministry of
housewives and farmers and merchants simply by announcing
it. It is necessary to *produce* it. The only way in which this
can be done is by the education of a gifted few, whose chief
vocation is the liberation of the ministerial and witnessing
power of the many. The major ministry of the pastors and

[10] *Life Is Commitment,* p. 98.

teachers, as made clear in Ephesians 4:12, is the "equipping ministry."[11]

The problem of *how* the ordinary Christian is to witness is one of such difficulty that it requires our best combined thought to have even the beginning of wisdom on the subject. We know that we must let our feeble light shine, that we must not be apologetic and cowardly; we know we must be ready to make the only contribution of any importance that we can—to give testimony to our own personal experience; but *how?* To buttonhole people in the crowd is simply ineffective; to wear a cross or a yoke-pin is such a little thing as to seem almost trivial; to attend public worship involves no courage. Martyr and witness are essentially synonymous, and what probability of martyrdom is there for a citizen of a country which is nominally Christian?

We may as well face the fact that the witness which most contemporary Christians will ever make is bound to be undramatic. Frequently, it will not seem like witness at all to the person who makes it, though it may seem so to the one who benefits by it. As we consider what has been crucial in our own lives we become aware of the fact that most of the testimonies which have helped us have been virtually unconscious ones. I remember a word a man said long ago— a word which deepened my life immeasurably—and I go to him in gratitude, but he has absolutely no memory of the word or the incident. This is as it should be. In a group of twenty-five lay Christians meeting recently, each told what was the major influence which had helped him to move over from nominal Christianity to a committed faith. Every one of the twenty-five mentioned a *person*. Not one mentioned a public occasion. And the surprising part was that all of the

---

[11] This term has been used with great effectiveness by Robert Raines in his new book, *New Life in the Church* (New York: Harper & Brothers, 1961).

persons mentioned as thus effective in personal ministry were inconspicuous. Most of them had made a significant witness without knowing it.

It appears to us that it is more difficult to make a Christian witness in a Christian country than in a missionary land, and this may be true. For instance, it is possible in some parts of Africa for a man who enters into Christian marriage to make a very striking witness. This he does by carrying a burden on his head just as his wife does, thus encountering the ridicule of the many because of his supposedly unmanly behavior. One man who was photographed assisting his wife in this courageous fashion stopped to interpret the meaning of his act. We say that we wish we could perform some act in which the difference which Christianity makes were equally clear, but we are hard pressed to know what act it might be.

One of the few areas in which a courageous witness is possible today is that of racial brotherhood. Perhaps the most vivid memory of 1960 that Americans will keep is that of the television scene of a young man in New Orleans walking past a jeering mob and becoming the butt of obscene remarks as he took his little daughter to school. What is really humiliating is the recognition of how comparatively rare such courage is. As the *New Yorker* pointed out in "Talk of the Town," there were only two parents out of two thousand who made the bold witness.

The most common alternative to a Christian witness is not something derogatory to Christ's cause, but *silence*. The condemnation of most of us arises not from what we have said, but from what we have failed to say. We are, let us say, in a room in which we hear some person maligned when we have evidence that the person is wholly innocent of the charge made. This happens almost constantly, because men and women love to gossip. The easy thing, of course, is to let the matter pass while we keep still, salving our consciences by saying that we cannot get into every fight. But it is precisely in such situations that the real test comes. The question is not, Will you go to hear Bishop X preach? The question is, Will you defend him when, at the dinner party, it is freely asserted that he is a Communist sympathizer because he believes in foreign aid? One of the most searching of all Christian queries is, Are you careful of the reputations of others?

We do not have to wait until we know the whole truth about anything to make our witness. If we were to wait for this, we should wait forever. There is a paradox in the fact that we can bear witness to the truth without claiming to be possessors of it. The truth is bigger than our systems, yet we must give testimony to the little that we now see. I must risk my reputation on the point at which I am willing to stand, even though much beyond that point is hazy. Only as we are willing to declare where we *are* are we likely to go beyond this unsatisfactory point. It is in this spirit that testimony is able to reconcile the two moods which seem so deeply opposed: boldness and humility. We can never say, "This I know beyond a shadow of doubt," for that kind of certainty is not given to finite men. All we can say is that "we are persuaded." What we mean is that we are willing to stake everything upon the conviction. This is the significance of Marcel's great statement that "every testimony is based on a commitment and to be incapable of committing oneself is to be incapable of bearing witness."[12]

The evidence of the gospel is not primarily in some document but in the lives of Christ's followers. It is the modest persons who have heard Christ's call to involvement and who try, imaginatively, to respond, who constitute the proof that the gospel is true. Since the proof is never completed, each

[12] *The Philosophy of Existence,* p. 68.

person is important. Each is important because each can add, by some unique and irrevocable act, to the cumulative evidence.

There is, perhaps, no part of the gospel story more revealing than the portion of the Fourth Gospel describing the encounter between Christ and Pilate. The mood of the Roman was exactly the opposite to that of a martyr. He sought to avoid involvement by cowardly neutrality but became thereby more deeply guilty. In the course of the conversation Pilate heard Christ say, "For this I was born, and for this I have come into the world, to bear witness to the truth" (John 18:37). It was the vocation of Christ to bear witness to the *truth*; it is our vocation to bear witness to *Him*.

CHAPTER 4

The Strategy of Penetration

I hazard the prophecy that that religion will conquer which can render clear to popular understanding some eternal greatness incarnate in the passage of temporal fact.
—Alfred North Whitehead

Any careful reader of the Gospels is bound to be struck by the obvious effort of Christ to make His hearers understand the nature of His cause. The effort was marked by the tireless use of a great many figures. He told His little company that they were the *salt* of the earth, that they were the *light* of the world, that He had turned over the *keys* of the kingdom; He compared His own work to that of *bread* and of *water;* He said the kingdom was like *leaven;* He said He had come to cast *fire* on the earth. At first the variety of these figures is bewildering, but a powerful insight comes when we realize, suddenly, what they have in common. Each figure represents some kind of penetration. The purpose of the salt is to penetrate the meat and thus preserve it; the function of light is to penetrate the darkness; the only use of the keys is to penetrate the lock; bread is worthless until it penetrates the body; water penetrates the hard crust of earth; leaven penetrates the dough, to make it rise; fire continues only as it reaches new fuel, and the best way to extinguish it is to contain it.

The cumulative effect of all of these figures is almost over-whelming. In any case, they make absolutely clear what the function of Christ's company is meant to be. The Church is never true to itself when it is living *for* itself, for if it is chiefly concerned with saving its own life, it will lose it. The nature of the Church is such that it must always be engaged in finding new ways by which to transcend itself. Its main responsibility is always outside its own walls in the redemption of common life. That is why we call it a re-demptive society. There are many kinds of religion, but redemptive religion, from the Christian point of view, is always that in which we are spent on those areas of existence which are located beyond ourselves and our own borders. "Religion is not a form of experience existing separately from other forms of experience. It is the transformation of the whole of experience."[1]

The outgoing character of the Christian movement is of such crucial importance that when it is understood, many of our religious presuppositions are thereby altered or re-jected. One result of such understanding is the recognition of the complete ineptitude of the idea of a "churchgoer," mentioned in an earlier chapter. Christians may indeed *come in,* but they do so only that they may, in consequence, *go out,* and furthermore, that they may go out with greater effectiveness. The preposition used in describing Christ's own strategy is highly significant. "He called to him the twelve, and began to send them *out*" (Mark 6:7). The point is almost equally clear in the dispatch of the Seventy, whom He sent "on ahead of him" (Luke 10:1). Though it is discouraging to find how few of the millions of nominal Christians have even a slight comprehension of this, it is heartening to find it understood in some places. Thus, the

[1] Oldham, *Life Is Commitment,* p. 96.

Second Congregational Church of Grand Rapids prints, at the end of its order of events, in its weekly bulletin,

> The End of Worship—
> The Beginning of Service.

As we study carefully the strategy employed by Christ, we are forced to conclude that the crucial step was that by which disciples were turned into apostles. It was necessary, of course, to have disciples first, because there had to be some reservoir of human resources on which to draw before the actual penetration of the world could begin. Christ started by the individual enlistment of modest men in His little company, devoting Himself largely to their training and discipline. This is not very surprising, since many others, including Socrates, have had disciples. A disciple is a student or a follower and, if Christ had had merely disciples, His position in this regard would not have been radically different from that of John the Baptist. What is different is that all of the disciples in Christ's company were potential apostles or ambassadors. They were enlisted not that they might share in a separated fellowship, such as the Essene community associated with the Dead Sea Scrolls, but that they might become the fellowship of penetration of the ordinary world.

If this analysis is correct it bears closely on the question of what a Christian is meant to be in the twentieth century, as well as what Christians were in the first century. It means that no person is really a Christian at all unless he is an evangelist or is getting ready to be one. The person who supposes that he can be a Christian by observing a performance, whether of the Mass or anything else, has missed the whole idea. There is nothing wrong with watching a performance, providing the watching serves to make the daily apostleship more real, but there is terrible wrong in watching a perform-

ance whenever this serves as the *end*. The Church, however
large its buildings and however grand its ceremonies or
vestments, is a denial of Christ unless it is affecting the
world—in business and government and education and
many other segments of human experience.

The Church can never be loyal to Christ merely by the
orthodoxy of its teaching about theology. The Apostle
Paul's most shocking heresy is not about theology, for in this
field he helped to establish orthodoxy, but rather it is his
bland rejection of those who were trying to criticize the
institution of slavery.[2] We are grateful that the essential
leaven of the gospel finally penetrated the worldly dough
sufficiently to make it possible for Christians to mount an
attack upon slavery, but the sorrow is that it took almost
eighteen hundred years for this operation to mature. The
gospel proved finally its penetrating power, but it was dis-
couragingly slow.[3]

In many contemporary Christian congregations the entire
church operation points to a climax on Sunday morning,
a conception which would have seemed very strange indeed
to the early Christians. Often the major effort during the
week is promotion of *Sunday,* the printed church paper
plugging constantly for a bigger attendance. Sunday morning, then, when it finally comes, has something of the mood
of a much advertised athletic contest, for which the team
has prepared and to which it has been pointed all week.
Finally, at twelve o'clock on Sunday, the whistle blows, the
climactic event is over for another week, and the spectators
go home to relax. If any reader imagines that this is a caricature, he ought to study the promotional material put out by
countless churches—material which gives the undeniable
impression that, for the Christian, the week is a preparation

[2] See I Timothy 6:1-6.
[3] On this point see Whitehead, *Adventures of Ideas.*

for Sunday. This is a complete reversal of the Christian pattern and something which finds no support whatever in the New Testament. The Christian pattern, if taken seriously, means exactly the opposite—namely, that what happens on Sunday is defensible only as a preparation for the daily ministry of the week which follows.

Worship is important, but it tends to be overemphasized in the contemporary church. It is very easy for the emphasis on worship to become a throwback to the Temple rather than a pushing forward to the strategy of Christ as represented in the Valiant Seventy. After all, it is significant to remember that Christ could contemplate the destruction of the Temple with absolute equanimity, and that, according to the record, when Jesus died on the cross "the curtain of the temple was torn in two" (Luke 23:45). The old order, which had served its day, was gone, and thereafter the "Seventy" was a more relevant symbol than the "Holy of Holies." What we have in the Bible is a threefold dialectic in which the Temple is the first moment, the synagogue the second moment, and the universal apostolate the third moment. The sorrow is that the Church is always tempted to slip back into one or the other of the positions which Christ came to transcend. There is a tendency, for example, to forget that Christ rejected the idea of a shrine as a necessary physical center of religious experience. This is the clear point of His unequivocal answer to the question of the Samaritan woman. "The hour is coming," He said, "when neither on this mountain nor in Jerusalem will you worship the Father" (John 4:21). Worship for the follower of Christ, whatever its details, can never be a matter of *place*.

If we were to take the idea of a militant company seriously, the church building would be primarily designed as a drill hall for the Christian task force. It would be a place where Christian ambassadors in common life would come together to be trained, to strengthen one another, and to find solitude when it is needed. The building might reasonably resemble the plan of a small college, with much emphasis upon the Christian library, the book store, the seminar rooms. It would be equipped with sleeping accommodations for the constant stream of visiting recruits and with an easily accessible quiet room. It would be armory, arsenal, barracks, and college, all in one. In short, it would resemble the new Christian centers which are beginning to appear in many part of the country.[4]

It is discouraging to see how slow churches are to make their church buildings contemporary. They seem to suppose that they are doing so when they adopt modernistic architectural design, but this is obviously a superficial and sometimes a foolish gesture. What is far more important than the use of peculiar lighting is a reconsideration of what the true function of a Christian building may be, and this depends, in turn, upon the philosophy of the nature of a Christian society. If the Church is an end in itself, one kind of building is reasonable, but if the Church is the apostolate, another kind is required. Since we have to use figures of speech, as the Church has always had to do, we may say that the Christian building should be a "launching pad," a place from which people engaged in secular life are *propelled*. The building is best understood not primarily as a shrine, and not as an assembly hall, but as the "headquarters" of the company. By a singular foresight, doing better than they realized, the members of the Church of the Saviour in Washington, D.C., when they purchased the modest building which they now occupy, began by calling it simply "Headquarters of the

[4] Two of the newest and most imaginative are Laity Lodge near Leakey, Texas, and Tri-State Yokefellow House near Defiance, Ohio. These houses welcome groups of many sizes as well as individuals at all times. Both are devoted to the revitalization of the Church in the surrounding regions.

Church of the Saviour." It is not called the "church," and it is not even the major scene of operations. The major scenes are the psychiatric clinic, the coffee house, the art center, and the factory for the unemployed.

The earliest Christians owned no buildings at all, and with very good reason: they were so deeply engaged in the task of penetrating the world that they had no time to build a monument to themselves. The oldest known Christian structures—those underground at Rome—date from about A.D. 250. When Christians did finally begin to build, their major pattern was the dwelling house rather than the shrine. This was reasonable in view of the New Testament expression "the church in their house."[5] There is nothing wrong with beauty, and we may be truly gratified for the labor which has gone into some ecclesiastical buildings, such as the medieval cathedrals, but we must never let even their beauty cause us to forget what the main purpose of a Christian building is. What we can say with real confidence is that a building designed to be used only once or twice a week is wholly inadequate. We need spiritual laboratories, with all of the emphasis placed on simple beauty and daily function rather than upon ostentation, or display. We have made a great start when we see the church building not as a holy place, but as the headquarters of the company, from which the recruits are expected to go *out*.

The effective Christian pattern is always a *base* and a *field*. The base—whether it be in a private house or in a church building—is the center to which the soldiers of Christ repair, periodically, for new strength. The field is the world, and this is where Christians are supposed to operate. A splendid and much admired example of this pattern is that instituted by Columba when he began the Christian invasion of Scotland nearly fourteen centuries ago, an example which, to some

[5] See I Corinthians 16:19 and Colossians 4:15.

degree, has been copied by the Iona Fellowship of our own generation. In Columba's imaginative conception, the beautiful island of Iona was the base while the mainland of Scotland was the field. The return of the workers to Iona was always temporary, because that was not the primary scene of operation. It was the point of departure and subsequent return, but the return was made only in order that there might be another departure. The men who now go to the island in the summer, participating there in the actual physical building of the needed structures, are expected to spend all of the remainder of each year on the mainland in the mission of penetration, particularly of industrial areas.

An undue pride in the grandeur of the building is by no means the only danger which arises when a single aspect of Christianity is emphasized disproportionately. Another equal but different danger arises from the nurture of the small prayer group. While there can be no doubt that the rediscovery of the power of the small group has been one of the genuine Christian advances in our generation, it is possible that the prayer group, like the sanctuary, *may* involve a retreat from reality. A prayer group is dangerous, and even harmful, if the members are satisfied to indulge in their own delightful fellowship, making this fellowship essentially an end in itself. The society of a little group of fellow believers can be so pleasant that the poverty and the sorrow of the outside world are forgotten, at least for the time of meeting. But the poverty and the sorrow must never be forgotten, not even for a little while. A prayer group which does not make its members more effective apostles in their jobs and homes, and more sensitive participators in the fellowship of those who bear the mark of frustration, is essentially a failure. The test of the vitality of a group does not occur primarily while the group is meeting; it occurs after the meeting is over.

The vitality of the original Christian movement was not demonstrated by the meetings they held, of which we have some limited knowledge, but by the way in which Christians provided an antidote to the loss of nerve and to the moral sag of the ancient world. If contemporary Christians are to have anything like the effect on modern civilization that Boris Pasternak[6] says early Christians had on Roman civilization, we shall have to do a great deal more creative dreaming than we do now, in order to discover *how*.

All who care deeply about the Christian cause are heartened when they hear of imaginative new ways in which penetration is occurring. One of the most successful of the new efforts is the establishment of The Potter's House in Washington, D.C. The Potter's House is a Christian coffee house, located by careful design in an area in which many young people are living in boardinghouses or apartments, and where the races tend to meet. The building is not marked by religious symbols, but looks, from the outside through the big windows, like a clean, attractive place in which to spend some time over a cup of coffee. Though it was established and is supported by a local church, it is never used as a means of promoting that church's attendance or membership or finance. People simply drop in, sip their coffee, talk, look at exhibits, and go out.

The members of the supporting church take turns at the task of being in The Potter's House each evening, waiting on tables, sitting with the guests, and being inconspicuous parts of the crowd. If a conversation about Christ and His cause starts, the members feel free to enter into it, but they

---

[6] See the paragraph from *Doctor Zhivago* quoted on pp. 15, 16. It is a curious fact that one of the most convincing descriptions of the redemptive penetration of the fellowship of the Living Christ should have been written in our time not by someone on our side of the Iron Curtain, but by that tragic genius who, though he was awarded the Nobel Prize, was forced by his fellow Russians to decline the honor.

never start it. They listen to complaints, to attacks, to expressed bitterness, to arrogant sophistry; they listen with patience, and they answer as well as they can, mindful of the glorious admonition, "Always be prepared to make a defense to any one who calls you to account for the hope that is in you, yet do it with gentleness and reverence" (I Peter 3:15).

The result of this program is that many disrupted and uprooted people of all ages, who would never knowingly enter a building labeled religious, will actually enter such a building. For the first ten months of operation the customers at The Potter's House averaged ten thousand a month. The consequent changes in some lives is phenomenal. Many people, as a result of long hours in this particular setting, now have a wholly new understanding of what the Church as a redemptive movement really is. Some have been able to emancipate themselves from adolescent censoriousness, as they begin to look, with growing humility, at the miraculous effectiveness of the Church of Jesus Christ through the ages. Their minds are freed from the antagonism to a particular kind of physical structure and from the identification of the Church with a clerical hierarchy. Some, when they learn that the members of the Church give their services without pay, many hours each week, are at first skeptical, then astonished, and then open. They can hardly believe it when they realize that this free gift of labor is what makes the solvency of the entire enterprise possible. They wonder at first what the "catch" is, watching confidently for the hook within the bait, but finally they are forced to admit that none exists.

Another powerful example of actual penetration is the work of some contemporary Christian groups in prisons. We have long had chaplains in prisons, both state and federal, and there has been no dearth of "services" conducted for the sake of the inmates, but in 1955 an entirely new pattern began to appear. It started in the McNeil Island Federal Penitentiary in the State of Washington, under the inspired leadership of Chaplain Charles F. Paine.[7] The prisoners formed a small redemptive group in which they, instead of being attenders at a service or listeners to the preaching of professionals, became themselves a fellowship of penetration within the prison. They moved quickly from the role of disciples to that of apostles, providing within the prison community a remarkable example of what may paradoxically be termed redemptive infection. The change in the men of the group was remarkable not only while they stayed behind prison walls; it has carried over into their lives as paroled or free persons as well.

Once the experiment at McNeil Island was generally known, it was quickly copied in other penal institutions, with similar effect. One of these institutions was the famous California prison at San Quentin, where the chief instigator was Cecil Osborne, a pastor of a Baptist church in Burlingame. Into the San Quentin Yokefellow group of twelve men there came a young prisoner. Already serving his third term, both of his former paroles having ended in forgery and other crimes, he was, by his own account, full of self-loathing which he naturally projected on others, including his fellow prisoners. When he entered the group of twelve for the first time, he was amazed at what he found. As a true novelty in his life he discovered the reality of love, because the other prisoners seemed actually concerned for *him*. With them he found he could share his feelings of self-loathing and his hatred for the lucky people who lived outside the prison gate. Like the other members of the group, the young forger learned to study the Scriptures with absolute regularity, and to pray by name for the other members of the group. At the

---

[7] See William L. Worden, "They Wear the Yoke Behind Prison Walls," in *Together*, August 1958.

same time he sought to extend the new life he experienced to the entire prison population, insofar as that was humanly possible. For the first time in his life he learned what it is to be concerned genuinely for someone other than himself. The result was that he became a new and truly liberated person. He learned that "when anyone is united to Christ, there is a new world; the old order is gone, and a new order has already begun" (II Corinthians 5:17, New English Bible).

Because of his new Christian experience the prisoner was ready for the risk of a third parole, but this parole was not granted until a similar group outside the prison—the group at Burlingame—sponsored him. At Burlingame the church members got him a self-respecting job, and he immediately joined one of the Yokefellow groups in the church—a prayer group that was more than a prayer group in that it practiced the strategy of penetration. *The miracle was that it had been able to penetrate even prison walls,* the walls of San Quentin. The paroled man reluctantly told the group the sad story of his past, and to his surprise they showed him a deeper affection rather than the rejection he expected. He had not reckoned with the power of Christian love. The San Quentin forger went on to become a student in the Berkeley Baptist Divinity School.

Let those who malign the Church ignorantly and unmercifully ponder the San Quentin story! There may be members of the Burlingame church who are mere attenders at a ceremony. But this we know: there are some others who see their function as Christians in terms of the penetration of the darkness by the light of Christ.[8] They are not satisfied, as they may once have been, with a mere "disciple plan"; they have proceeded to the acceptance of an "apostle plan." They may be imperfect, but they have caught a glimpse of the

[8] See "Commitment to Life," in *Crusader*, December 1960, pp. 6 ff.

dynamic logic of Christ beginning with *commitment,* which, if it is real, involves *enlistment,* which demands the kind of *witness* which leads to *penetration.*

The coffee house experiment and the prison experiment, though they are very striking, are only two of many experiments in the penetration of common life now being conducted. Most of these receive little publicity, and sometimes they are not even known to church leaders or to those who write about the strength and weakness of the Christian cause.[9]

One highly imaginative example of a penetrating Christian movement is the Fellowship of Christian Athletes.[10] This fellowship conducts summer conferences for college and high school athletes at both Estes Park, Colorado, and Lake Geneva, Wisconsin, but it is by no means limited to such efforts. The movement started with the observation that young men care about athletic prowess, that they are bound to have athletic heroes, and that great changes may come in their lives if these heroes are men of intelligent faith.

Nearly all of the strong movements of Christian laymen are now so organized that they emphasize not Sunday religion, but the effect of the gospel upon secular professions and daily work. We have some Christian leaders who, if they have to choose between speaking to a church audience and speaking to a meeting of the bar association, will choose the latter. They do this because they know that the leaven is ineffective unless it actually gets into the lump. The tragedy of many religious audiences is that they have become

[9] For example, no mention is made of such experiments by Russell Kirk in his article "Can Protestantism Hold Its Own in a Modern America?" in *Fortune,* February 1961, pp. 108 ff. Even more surprising is the omission of reference to such experiments on the part of Martin E. Marty in *The New Shape of American Religion* (New York: Harper & Brothers, 1959).

[10] The headquarters of the Fellowship of Christian Athletes is in Kansas City, Mo. The executive director is Don McClanen.

immunized by much listening to speeches. Wise Christian leaders will not give their precious time to saving the saved when they have alternative opportunities in life outside the purview of the Church. Such men, if they are writers, will choose to place articles in *The Saturday Evening Post* or *Reader's Digest* or *The Atlantic Monthly,* in preference to a religious journal. Certainly they will not write primarily with the intention of impressing fellow theologians. This follows naturally if they have even a vague notion of what the strategy of penetration means. "Writers, if they are worthy of that jealous name," says Archibald MacLeish, "do not write for other writers."[11]

When we begin to get a new vision of the Church as a fellowship seeking to reach into every nook and cranny of common life, we start looking for really fresh ways of operating in faithfulness to our inner mission. New subsidiary associations devoted to mutual help in hard but needed tasks are bound to spring up. One such group is the Guild of Christian Writers, an association of men and women who encourage and assist one another, particularly by the criticism of one another's literary work. Several good books have been published which would never have been written apart from this creative fellowship. Always, the purpose is to help one another in the effort to write in such a manner that modern man will listen. It is not enough for a scholar to empty his desk drawer into a pretentious volume. Great discipline, in regard to style as well as content, must be learned if we really seek to reach contemporary minds and are not satisfied merely to have books published. Among the features to be considered carefully is length, a feature to which C. S. Lewis has obviously paid close attention. There is little point, he seems to have understood, in printing what no one will read, no matter how important its message may be.

[11] In *Saturday Review,* Nov 26, 1960, p. 26.

Just as we have a Guild of Christian Writers who assist one another, regardless of their fields of interest, we need a Guild of Christian Politicians. Such a guild might be composed of young men who know something of where power for good resides in the modern world and who propose to do something about it by helping one another—both to get ready and to operate when they *are* ready. Each man is almost helpless alone, but together they might do wonders. They would stand at the opposite pole from those sincere but misguided Christian groups who suppose that a Christian cannot even vote, much less hold office. The fault in their understandable position is that they automatically create a power vacuum which others—perhaps less qualified or less conscientious—are sure to fill. The young men in the ideal Guild of Christian Politicians will not meet exclusively for prayer, though they may pray; they will meet to raise one another's sights, to stimulate, to advise, to learn. We must remember that while thought may be *developed* in privacy, it is seldom *engendered* in that way. We are creatures who need one another, especially in all intellectual endeavors. That is the essential reason for the artificial societies called colleges.

Among the needed new societies are those to be created specifically for the intelligent effort to recover the lost provinces of the contemporary Church. It is not enough to look upon the entire Church as one mighty company; we must also form subsidiary companies, or Christian task forces, to which specific assignments can be made.

A most urgently needed task force is one to restore Christian vitality in the colleges and universities, from which it has so largely departed. It must be understood that such an undertaking is no light matter—that at best the campaign will be long or unending and that the opposition is as strong as it is vocal. Because the belligerent hostility of semieducated youth to any religion is far greater than we like to admit, the persons enrolled in this force need a preparation that is awesomely thorough. When so much of the opposition appeals, though erroneously, to science, the members of this subcompany must be knowledgeable about science and skilled in scientific method.[12] And since so many of the current problems are those with which the great philosophers have always been concerned, these campaigners must know philosophy. They must know *enough* philosophy not to be unduly impressed by the arrogance of a logical positivist.

The standard argument against Christianity today combines scientism, positivism, and determinism. Our best strategy, of course, is attack, and determinism is the first point on which we can train our workers to attack. This is the best place to begin because the philosophical position of determinism is so obviously vulnerable. The determinist can be shown to be undermining even his own logical position and therefore his own determinism, for in a world in which every action is predetermined the whole conception of truth and falsity becomes meaningless. Each person—who, according to the determinist position, is nothing but a pawn—does what he must and that is the end of the matter, but this is bound to include the believer in the truth of determinism as well as everyone else. At the same time it can be shown to any really open-minded person that a belief in determinism makes impossible any genuine responsibility. I am certainly not to blame for what I cannot help doing. This may seem elementary, but there are thousands of students in our colleges today who have not even considered such points. The task of the Christian is not to engage in pious talk, but rather

[12] A good example of a powerful counterattack occurs at Carleton College, where the head of the Religion Department, Professor Ian Barbour, teaches the course in atomic physics. Professor Barbour is a Ph.D. in physics who took postdoctoral work at Yale Divinity School. This combination, while highly desirable, is understandably rare.

to discipline his mind to outthink all opposition, expecting no quarter and asking none. If the Christian faith cannot bear full examination, it will be the first time in nineteen hundred years that this has been the case.

Always, the way to recover lost territory, academic or otherwise, is to accept the challenge rather than to neglect it. A good example of such strategy may be seen in the Christian's reaction to the atheistic existentialism of Jean Paul Sartre. We should start with Sartre, for here we have a point of contact, in his brave acceptance of personal responsibility, which contrasts so nobly with all determinism. All that we ask of a man like Sartre is that he examine carefully what the concept of responsibility implies. To whom am I responsible? It is clear that responsibility is a concept which is intrinsically transitive in character; it requires an *object*. Since things are not responsive and cannot be, only a personal object makes sense. But I cannot reasonably be responsible to myself, for I am not good enough to warrant it. The same is true of any other finite person or group of finite persons. Therefore, if responsibility is to be understandable, it must involve responsibility to Almighty God, for only in God is there the adequate personality and worthiness. It is possible—and even likely—that many of those existentialists who are also atheists would not be willing to follow this logical procedure, but they at least deserve the opportunity of examining it. It would be the function of a Christian academic task force to meet such opposition, to take it seriously, and to go on from there. But the ability to do so cannot come from taking an easy course.

In the long run the best solution of the problem of a fragmented and secularized education is the development of a Guild of Christian Professors who are equally skilled in some secular field of learning and in the unapologetic support of the Christian view of reality. Such people, who may teach geology or psychology or physics or anything else in the entire academic curriculum, can, if they will, become the spearhead of the Christian movement in even the most secularized of universities. It also seems, to our sorrow and shame, they are now needed equally in some of the institutions founded and supported by Christian conviction.

One of our urgent needs is to find men who can go to colleges and universities for what is called religious emphasis week. This work is so grueling and requires powers so unusual that the only hope lies in training persons specifically for the task. They must be prepared to lecture, to lead symposiums, to meet individual seekers at all hours, to listen to ancient objections with respectful attention, and to present the truth of Christ persuasively. The persons who can learn to do all this will not be under any delusion that skeptics can be argued into the kingdom, but they will know that there are thousands kept *out* of the kingdom by some little barrier or misgiving that can be handled with comparative ease, providing the missioner is ready. A good example of the beneficent elimination of such a barrier concerns the idea of God as truly personal. A girl says she cannot think of God as personal, though Christ obviously did, because God seems to her a great cosmic "force." Part of her motivation is that she is very eager not to have her idea of God too small or, as she would say, anthropomorphic. The member of the academic task force, if he understands his business, can show the girl that in her effort to avoid limiting God she has done exactly what she has sought to avoid. If *she* can know her friend and God *cannot* know him, this means that God is incapable of something of undoubted worth. The upshot is that she is really imposing a limit on God. The odd consequence is that the creature is recognized as greater, at one point, than the Creator. Suddenly the girl may see this with clarity and, as a result, gain a grateful sense of intellectual relief. The point is that she cannot do it alone; she needs help; and it is the work of the Christian professor, whatever subject he may teach, to provide that help.

What has been said about work in academic institutions can be extended to the recovery of vitality in other lost provinces, such as youth in general and organized labor. We need a new kind of center in which the skills for these task forces are deliberately cultivated. One might suppose that this is done in the standard theological seminaries, but, for the most part, it is not consciously done anywhere. This is one of the reasons why we need to take a new hard look at theological education. Too often, the seminary curriculum is a matter of going through the ancient motions, whereas it ought to do for the Christian cause something as bold as that which is done for the Communist cause in the Lenin Institute of Russia. That Institute makes a deliberate attempt to prepare men to occupy new territory. We have a different conception of what occupation of either new or old territory means, but we need to be equally serious in the effort. The preparation, if it is to be adequate, will not be less arduous.

We do not know much about how to reach modern youth, but we know a few things. One thing we know is that the policy of merely entertaining the young people in the church building does not and cannot succeed. What does succeed, in some places, is a venture in intellectual depth. Thus, in Midland, Michigan, a young Ph.D. in chemistry who is employed by the Dow Chemical Company is conducting a study of the hardest problems in the philosophy of religion, and he is conducting it among juniors and seniors in Midland High School! The class meets in homes on Sunday evenings and sometimes continues, with great enthusiasm, for as long as three hours at a time. Whether this can be duplicated in other places we do not know, but the fact that it can be done anywhere is highly reassuring. In any case, we need special institutes in which the task of reaching youth is studied with all of the intelligence which we can muster and from which the members of the institute are sent out to put their specific skills into practice. That this is a far cry from the old-fashioned training in religious education is obvious. Nearly all of the new tactics are still to be learned, but they will not be learned unless we form bodies designed for this very purpose. The holding of youth is so important for the Church of Jesus Christ that if we were wise we should jointly and imaginatively try to discover how it can be accomplished.

In a similar way we must have imaginative joint studies on how to reach labor. We must enlist the assistance of those few who are convinced followers of Christ and also members of labor unions. We have some splendid books on Christianity and daily work, but not books from men actually engaged in organized labor.[13] We have had fine words about the possible dignity of daily work, but it is doubtful if much of this has reached the rank and file. "Why should a scientist or an engineer or an administrator," asks J. H. Oldham, "attach any great importance to religion unless it says to him: 'In the work you are doing day by day you are a partner with God in His work of creation and the realization of His purpose for the family of the sons of men.' "[14] Can ordinary workers learn to say this?

We must, before it is too late, find ways to get to the men on the production line. It is a fact that the Christian faith does have a valid answer to the problem of the dullness of factory work, in the sense of a man becoming a partner in God's creation, even in little things, but what good does this do if it is not known or appreciated? Special preparation,

[13] Good examples of books on work written by intellectuals are John Oliver Nelson, ed., *Work and Vocation* (New York: Harper & Brothers, 1954); and Alexander Miller, *Christian Faith and My Job* (New York: Association Press, 1959).
[14] *Life Is Commitment,* p. 109.

which is not now provided anywhere, is required for the work of a labor task force. Certainly the ordinary preparation for the ordinary pastorate is not adequate or even relevant. For one reason, the mission to labor may not involve any *preaching* at all. It may involve a contemporary version of the worker-priest idea which, though it has been abandoned in France, may still be valid. Or there may be some new way to be discovered of which we have not even dreamed. If we were to have Christian research in such a field, as Dupont and Dow Chemical have in scientific fields, it is not unlikely that some really fresh answers would appear.

It need hardly be said that all of these new contemporary tasks are so arduous that they will never appeal to those who want easy lives or who desire to follow only in well-tried and conventional Christian channels. Many of the experiments in these new areas will fail, as scientific experiments frequently do, but that is how progress is possible. In any case, herein lies the relevant ministry for our time, and someone must begin the preparation for it. It is just possible that the very boldness of the undertaking, with consequent lack of security, may attract some strong minds, as the dangerous vocation of the astronaut has already attracted so many bold men. In only a few schools is the conventional professional ministry attracting the strongest recruits today, but, with a new vision, there could be a radical change.

What we need to do is to consider the tasks which are most urgent for our time and then try to find the men and women who will get ready to perform them. In Russia the two groups which now seem to have attracted the ablest persons are the grade school teachers and the engineers. They are given great prestige and a relatively high income as an incentive. One possible result is that the Russians *may* supersede us in the development both of human talent and of the machines which provide such power. If we who care about the Church and its farflung ministry were boldly wise, perhaps we should give much greater incentive to work with youth than we give to the management of a big ecclesiastical organization. But we cannot do this, or anything remotely similar, unless we have a revolutionary change in our own vocational values.

Once we begin to alter our conception of what the Church is, viewing it as intrinsically missionary—not merely in Africa, but in every part of the life of the West as well— we realize that we have hardly begun to see what our major task is. If we produce and train Christian task forces for universities and for youth and for labor, why should we stop there? We must have new approaches to the problems of poverty, of mental illness, of leisure, and many more. The horizon of Christian work will ever expand, for in the kingdom there is no known limit.

The expanding horizon of the ministry of all Christians seems to be the burden of Christ's last recorded words on the earth. The last words of Christ are found, not in any of the Synoptic Gospels nor in John, but in the first chapter of the Acts of the Apostles. The last words that Christ was heard to say, after His death and resurrection, were these: "You shall be my witnesses in Jerusalem and in all Judea and Samaria and to the end of the earth." What final testament could be more clear? The purpose of one enlisted in Christ's service is to penetrate concentric circles to the farthest border. The method of penetration is witness. By making witness we go "into all the world," including those aspects of the world called government and law and business and home life and scholarship. Thus the final words of Christ combine, in a single formula, the theme of witness and the theme of penetration. If the witness is to penetrate, as our culture requires, the major witness must be made not in the Church but in the world.

Herein lies the significance of the haunting words of Whitehead, which are used as the epigraph of this chapter, to which so many have responded. It is primarily in the passage of temporal fact—in the work of laboratories and factories, in the love of parents and children, in the discipline of secular minds, in the discoveries of new medicines and new ways of eliminating degrading poverty—that the true glory of the Living God is to be seen, if it is to be seen anywhere. It is not that there are two valid religions, one of the Holy of Holies and the other of common life. The truth is, as Whitehead saw and said so well, that there is only one valid religion, the religion by which the potential glory of common life is liberated and revealed.

CHAPTER 5

The Criterion of Validity

The loves we had were far too small.
—Stephen Vincent Benét

The best way to understand what the Church ought to *do* is to try to understand what the Church *is*. The partially realized or even unrealized dream is our most precious possession because it shows us where we fail and helps us, accordingly, to see the direction in which we ought to be moving. In the preceding chapters we have sought to depict important features of the essential Church, but something of even greater importance has been omitted. We have stressed the idea of a witnessing society which generates great propulsive power, and this the Church has always been in its periods of health, but the idea so stated is manifestly incomplete. After all, the Communist religion involves a fellowship, elicits unquestioning dedication, upholds its position by enduring martyrdom, and is remarkably successful in penetrating many parts of the social order. Why, then, from the Christian point of view, is it not adequate? Any attempt to answer this question takes us to the very center of the Christian faith, including the redemptive society which we call the Church.

The marks of a true Church, as against spurious versions,

have attracted the attention of Christian thinkers from the beginning. The necessity of such consideration is obvious to us when we think how easy it is to let a religion become debased. All students of the history of religion are conscious of developments which amount to genuine perversion. The New Testament Epistles refer to early deviations, and even Christ Himself predicted that many would fall away (Matthew 24:10). Though the attempts to draw a line of authenticity have been numerous in Christian history, there are, today, six major efforts to present a single criterion of validity for a true Church of Christ. In each case, all who fail to meet the particular criterion are ruled out as not meeting the full conditions of membership.

One familiar answer to the question of the criterion of validity is communion with, or subservience to, the Bishop of Rome. By this arbitrary standard, if a Church has this human connection it is a valid Church, and if it does not it is heretical or lacking in genuineness. This answer is fundamentally simple, and easily understood, but suffers from the vital defect that it has no support whatever from the known words of Christ or from His earliest followers. The idea of a pope is simply not a New Testament idea at all.[1] The notion that one group has a spiritual monopoly represents a fundamental break with the spirit of Christ, insofar as that is known by His recorded words. We may, therefore, dismiss it.

In like manner we must reject the test of Apostolic Succession, in the sense that an unbroken laying on of hands from bishop to bishop through the years is some sort of guarantee. The fact that one man touches the body of another man is obviously trivial and one which gives no guarantee whatever of the continuation of a spirit. When people

[1] The frequent attempts to base it upon Matthew 16:18 cannot survive careful examination or logical analysis.

depart from Christ it is not difficult to depart farther and farther, while priding themselves on a supposed continuity. Each step may be small, but the accumulated divergence may be tremendous. What is far more important than organizational continuity is the integrity which can come from drinking again at the Source. We know that men can be true ministers of Christ without sacerdotal ordination because they actually *do* minister, and they demonstrate their genuineness by their fruits.

A third test is that of Biblical literalism, according to which acceptance of every word of our present Bible is seen as the criterion of a true Church. We can see the falsity of this test at once when we realize that it was not even a possible one in the early Church because many of the books, to which adherence is now required, had not yet been written. Absolute Biblical literalism, while upheld as a dogma by some, is in fact impossible and is never seen in practice. Subjective interpretations are always added to force consistency. Even an appearance of consistency is not possible except by virtue of ingenious dodging, which some denominations have made into an art. Some of the churches in which this test is upheld actually have women speakers. They try to avoid the embarrassment of Paul's admonition that women should keep silence in the churches, by saying that the Apostle referred only to a local situation, but, when they adopt this facile solution of their problem, they have to forget the fact that Paul plainly universalized his injunction (I Corinthians 14:33 ff.).

A fourth familiar test of a true Church is freedom from certain personal habits such as dancing or theatergoing. Though the emphasis on this criterion is well intentioned, it means a return to a pre-Christian or Pharisaic position. We ought to make our lives as virtuous as we can make them, but it is perfectly clear that the Church, as Christ envisaged it, is not limited to those who are primarily concerned with keeping their own skirts clean. The author of the book of James could write about the ideal of keeping oneself "unstained from the world" (1:27), but there is no counterpart of this Puritan ideal in the recorded teachings of Jesus or in the reputation which Jesus gained. We are told that He deliberately risked what looked like stain by His association with such people as prostitutes. Christ understood the danger, for He knew that the popular gossip was "Behold, a glutton and a drunkard, a friend of tax collectors and sinners!" (Luke 7:34). In the light of this evidence we conclude that the true Church of Jesus Christ can never be limited to the righteous; it is for those who are broken and who know that they are broken. "I came," He said, "not to call the righteous, but sinners" (Mark 2:17).

A fifth proposal concerning the criterion of validity in the Church is that of a creedal formulation. Adherence to a particular creed, whether the Apostles' Creed or the Nicene Creed or some other, is frequently proposed as the crucial test, with the consequent exclusion of many. No serious Christian can consider these great creeds without reverent respect, and only the confused suppose that belief is unimportant, but when we make the creedal test the crucial one we distort the Christian picture completely. It is not enough —nor even necessary—to say "Lord, Lord." Every human creed is inadequate, not only because it tends to harden what ought to be fluid and living, but, what is worse, because it fails to catch the full significance of commitment.[2]

A sixth proposal of a criterion is ceremonial. Strange as it may appear, there are Christians who hold that a person is not really a member of Christ's Church unless he has submitted to some particular ceremony. There is only one

---

[2] The Apostles' Creed and the Nicene Creed both involve a partial element of commitment by the use of "I believe *in*."

true Church and theirs is it! That such arrogance is possible among persons who claim to be loyal followers of Christ is almost unbelievable, but it occurs, and it seems to be able to elicit remarkable zeal. If this phenomenon were to appear in some other faith we should not be so surprised, but it actually appears in the supposed effort to follow Christ who said that what is outside a man is insignificant (Mark 7:15) Christ clearly broke with every emphasis on holiness by means of foods or anything of an external nature. He welcomed to His eternal fellowship one of the thieves on the cross, when there was not even the possibility of any kind of ceremonial performance. Christ was concerned with reality and with nothing else, but there are always people who cannot rise to this level. They are still pre-Christian in their assumption that membership in Christ's true Church is limited by external performance. It is strange that they are not profoundly disturbed by the fact that Christ did not baptize and that some of His references to baptism, far from indicating an inflexible mode, seem to be highly spiritual. How else can they understand His haunting words, "I have a baptism to be baptized with; and how I am constrained until it is accomplished!" (Luke 12:50). Whatever He meant, He did not mean His baptism by John in the Jordan River, for that was already accomplished.

Loyalty to Christ does not mean that we *reject* those who still participate in ceremonial rites. Rites do not hurt people, and they may even help. Furthermore, mere absence of rites is no guarantee of spirituality or of Christian validity. It is *neither* circumcision nor lack of circumcision that counts, but a new creation in Christ (Galatians 6:15). What we must always oppose is the position of one who makes his own understanding of a rite the necessary door for all other men. He is adopting a means of exclusion for which there is no rational defense.

In the light of all of these insupportable criteria, we must beware at all points of the heresy of simplification, which is common to all of the six efforts to uphold a single criterion. Though they seem very different, they really have much in common. The failure of each is the failure to see the richness and the variety of the fellowship which the Church of Jesus Christ always exhibits when it stays close to its Source. The central error of each of the six marks is that each one is really too easy. There is no hope for the contemporary Church unless it is able to resist the temptation to oversimplification which makes a small and easily distinguishable mark the crucial one. The true Church is bigger and deeper than we know.

It is paradoxical, indeed, that each of the criteria which is popularly supported is concerned with something which Christ did not propose, while the criterion which He did propose seems not to have become the battle cry of any organized group. His own piercing words are: "By this all men will know that you are my disciples, if you have love for one another" (John 13:35). This sentence must not be taken alone, for Christ gave other commandments, such as the injunction to witness, but no sincere Christian can fail to take it seriously. It may not indicate the *sufficiency* of love, but it at least indicates the *necessity* of love. We know, then, whatever else we know, that the unloving fellowship is an heretical fellowship, so far as Christianity is concerned. How strange, in the light of the Biblical insistence on love as the principal thing, that we have emphasized it so little in comparison with other elements. We ask what Presbyterians *believe*, but we seldom ask how Presbyterians *love*. Heresy trials do not seem to be conducted with I Corinthians 13:13 in mind. Two of the Christian thinkers who have helped most, in the present century, to restore the balance of thought about the nature of the true Church are W. A. Visser 't Hooft and J. H. Oldham, both of whom had much to do with the formation of the World Council of Churches. They were especially helpful when they combined their insights by writing as joint authors. Their conclusion, as seen in the following sentences, ought to have the respectful attention of all who care about this crucial subject:

The Church has rightly laid stress on faith, since it is only by our personal response to God's personal call that we can be redeemed to a new life. But it has in a far less degree emphasized the other truth, that the new life into which we are called and admitted is a life of community and love. The impression which the Church has too often conveyed to the world is that to be a Christian means primarily to hold certain doctrinal beliefs. Only through the lives of some of its saints and a relatively small proportion of its humbler and unknown members has it given to the outside world occasion to suppose that to be a Christian is to be redeemed into a new sphere of being in which love and freedom reign.[3]

The nature of a true Christian society or Church is so rich that it cannot be fully expressed in a single idea. Love is not the only mark—it is merely the final mark. Though the marks of the true Church are many, a particular mark may, with logical consistency, be recognized as more important than the others. When we truly become a Company of Christ's Committed Ones we exhibit a number of features which fit together into a total complex of greater and lesser features. In such a society there is *commitment,* and *enlistment,* and *witness,* and *penetration* of common life, and *caring,* but the greatest of these is *caring.* The Church of Jesus Christ is not merely a society of love, for love is conceiv-

[3] W. A. Visser 't Hooft and J. H. Oldham, *The Church and Its Function in Society* (Chicago: Willett-Clark, 1937), pp. 146-47.

able in any historical tradition, but if the Church is genuine, it must always involve love as the most important single attribute.

Commitment, then, is not sufficient; we must be committed in a particular way. Our commitment is outside the spirit of Christ if it involves an effort to ride over other men, to use them for our cause, or to see anything else as more important than the individual welfare of individual persons. For the Christian faith, when it understands itself, there is only one absolute, and that absolute is the genuine *caring* which is expressed in the Greek word *agape*.

We know something when we know that, whatever the problem, we must always be truly loving. We do not know, in our finitude, which of various possible pathways is the really loving one, but the effort to discover it is an immense help. While the demand of love is always the major premise, we must use our common sense and reason and experience to know what the minor premise may be. I know I must be loving to the beggar who approaches me, but only reason can help me to know whether it is more loving to give him money or to withhold it and to help in some other way. In short, the recognition of the Christian absolute, while it gives us a firm base in principle, does not relieve us of the necessity of hard thinking.

In many ways the recognition that love is the final test of orthodoxy is shocking. It means that we may be outside the true fellowship of Christ even when we are ardent workers for some social improvement, if our crusade is carried on in an unloving way. Thus it is possible to have a burning zeal for race equality or for world peace that is really alien to Christ, provided the zeal allows us to be unloving or unfair to those who happen to differ from us on these particular issues. The paradox of the unloving pacifist, who condemns all of those in the armed forces and maligns

his opponents, is one which we sometimes see in contemporary experience. It may be no worse than many other features
of our religious life, but it stands out because the incon-
sistency of the position is so glaring. Christian pacifism is a
great and needed witness, but whenever it is separated from
the love of Christ it seems inevitably to become cruel and
bitter. The crusade for racial justice, with absolute insistence
upon equality of opportunity and equal justice, is one of the
most urgent matters in the life of modern man, but if it is
separated from love, even the demand for justice is debased.
A Negro's hatred of white people, while understandable, is
really no better than a white man's contempt for colored
people. The task of the Church is to be a continual reminder
of what the central matter is. The need of this is particularly
clear in the current crusade of militant anticommunism.
The leaders of this movement are right in opposing the
spread of the Communist conspiracy, but the Church must
refuse to be their protective front when they press their
crusade in unloving ways, including the maligning of those
with excellent reputations.

There is no reason to suppose that there was a single pattern of organization in the life of the early Church or a
single way of worship, but, whatever the variety, there was
a recurring emphasis upon the mutual love of the brethren.
The glorious poem on love, in the sense of caring, which is
imbedded in I Corinthians is indeed the highest point, but
it stands as one part of a mountain range and not as a single
isolated peak. The first Christians were sometimes divisive,
sometimes snobbish, sometimes deceitful, but they had no
doubt concerning the nature of the standard from which they
were departing. It was the standard of a loving concern for
one another and for all men, in the sense of a burning desire
for the welfare of the other person. Though most of the
early Christians were glaringly imperfect, the affectionate

quality of their fellowship was actually noted by the outside
world.

We know that the early Christians were sinful men and
women, because the New Testament provides much evidence
concerning the details of their sin, but we also know the
almost miraculous effect of their concern for one another.
The combinations of the term "fellow" are really very impressive, especially in the Epistles. In the one short book of
Philemon we find "fellow worker," "fellow soldier," and
"fellow prisoner." In Philippians there is the potent term
"yokefellow," as well as numerous expressions of affection
and thankfulness for "partnership in the gospel" (1:5). The
glorious fellowship, so vividly described in Acts, seems actually to have been infectious and to have carried over from
the Jerusalem group to those who lived in Asia Minor and
in Greece. We are today almost envious when we read how
our spiritual ancestors "devoted themselves to the apostles'
teaching and fellowship, to the breaking of bread and the
prayers" (2:42). The word "fellowship" may be somewhat
debased now, but then it was not.

The most remarkable single feature of the mutual concern
of the New Testament fellowship—its financial aspect—led
to what has been rightly termed "unlimited liability among
the members." The affection did not find its chief expression
in words, though words here as elsewhere were important,
but carried over to the extent that the members of the redemptive fellowship distributed to all, "as any had need" (Acts
2:45). One of the reasons for some of the abundant travel of
the early Christian leaders was the collection, transfer, and
delivery of financial help from one little group to an even
more needy group.[4] What was called a "contribution for the
saints" was the original form of subsequent Christian giving.
It arose, almost spontaneously, as a direct result of the potent

[4] See I Corinthians 16:1-4 and Acts 24:17.

concern for one another which the Christian fellowship involved.

If our only evidence of the early Christian concern for one another were that found in the New Testament it would be very impressive, but it is supplemented by many other sources. Few experiences would be more helpful to the contemporary Christian who sincerely wants to know what a Church might be, than a reading or a rereading of Harnack's great chapter "The Gospel of Love and Charity" in his *The Mission and Expansion of Christianity in the First Three Centuries*. "The new language on the lips of Christians," he writes, "was the language of love." Then he goes on to say, "But it was more than a language, it was a thing of power and action. The Christians really considered themselves brothers and sisters and their actions corresponded to this belief."[5]

The evidence of love as the ultimate mark and test of the Christian community comes from many post-Biblical sources. One of the most moving of all testimonies is Tertullian's:

It is our care for the helpless, our practice of lovingkindness, that brands us in the eyes of many of our opponents. "Only look," they say, "look how they love one another. . . . Look how they are prepared to die for one another."[6]

Justin Martyr supplements this witness, in the conclusion of his description of Christian worship, as follows:

Those who are well-to-do and willing, give as they choose, each as he himself purposes; the collection is then deposited with the president, who succours orphans, widows, those who are in want owing to sickness or any other cause, those who are in prison, and strangers who are on a journey.[7]

[5] Adolf Harnack, *The Mission and Expansion of Christianity in the First Three Centuries* (New York: G. P. Putnam's Sons, 2nd ed., 1908), Vol. I, p. 149.

[6] Tertullian, *Apolog.* xxxix.

[7] Justin, *Apolog.* c. lxvii.

As we look at the record, we see that the Christians of the early centuries of our era admitted both their failure and their standard. They accepted at its face value the declaration that the crucial, though not the sole, mark of the new society Christ founded—and the one which most clearly differentiated it from all others—was that its members were not masters, but servants. Though they were themselves inadequate and sinful men and women, they freely recognized that the Church exists in order to witness, and that the witness is meant to be a demonstration of the right relation of men with one another.

It must never be supposed that in a true Church the acceptance of responsibility is limited to fellow members. Indeed, in all of the great periods of vitality, the Church has been deeply concerned for the welfare of those who are not adherents at all. Love of the brethren is not inconsistent with love of the others, and a remarkable degree of outgoing affection is sometimes demonstrated. The worst cynic could hardly fail to be moved if he could go to one of the contemporary Christian fellowships, which he affects to despise, and watch a collection for people on another continent, not one of whom has ever been seen by the givers and whose only appeal to the givers is that they are children of a common Father, made equally in His image. Even where the fires of Christian commitment seem to have burned very low, there is still enough of a remaining emphasis on "inasmuch as ye did it to the least of these, my brethren" that the appeal for the needy has powerful unseen backing in even the most modest Christian congregation.

Part of our study of Christian history ought to be devoted not to doctrinal disputes, creedal formulations, heresies, and schisms, but to the finest examples of Christian love. By contemplating these we may be able to see what the standard from which we deviate really is, and we may have encouragement to go deeper. Thus, as we study the medieval Church and its doctrines, we must be sure to study *The Little Flowers of St. Francis,* because in these naïve and delightful stories we can catch some vision of what love of the brethren can be. Since there is no fixed limit to human ability, the only way in which we can know what is possible is to see what *has been.* Christianity has survived miraculously, in the midst of terrible dangers, chiefly because it has found concrete embodiment in human lives of persuasive quality, and the most persuasive of all qualities is that of genuine affection. One demonstration is worth a hundred arguments, for though doctrines may be impressive, it is experience that is convincing.

Among the great demonstrations one that is very convincing, though little known or studied, is that reported by Robert Barclay of Scotland. In his book *Truth Triumphant* Barclay describes the really exciting fellowship of imprisoned Christians in Aberdeen throughout the winter of 1677. Since the prison, or "Tolbooth," is still standing, we can picture the horror of the setting as the men and women sat in rooms lit only by narrow slits in heavy stone, their chains imbedded in the walls. What is wonderful is that the quality of affection which the imprisoned persons experienced in that dreadful winter had nothing whatever in common with the physical setting. We can still read with admiration and wonder the words Barclay wrote in March 1677 in Aberdeen Prison and to which he gave the inspiring title "Universal Love Considered."[8]

Once we reject the easier tests of validity we are better prepared to seek the changes necessary to make the contemporary Church a genuine one. As we look humbly for help in seeing the vision, we soon learn that it can come from

[8] Robert Barclay, *Truth Triumphant,* Vol. III, pp. 183 ff.

unexpected and unconventional quarters. For example, we can receive valuable assistance from Alcoholics Anonymous. This association, which has exhibited undiminished vitality for more than a quarter of a century, is really a living witness to what loving fellowship can be and, unintentionally, a judgment upon the Church as a whole. How strange that it took those who were struggling with compulsive drinking to remind us of something which most of the existent Church had forgotten!

The many groups called A. A. teach us that the deepest fellowship can be based upon a sense of tragic need, and that the vitality of the fellowship is maintained by unending service to one another. Every member is constantly on call, day and night; a new member is telephoned and visited every day for a long period because the danger of slipping is always present, particularly in the trial period. Each member who feels the approach of danger in his own life immediately tries to aid another and, in his concern for the other person, his own problem is often solved. In his effort to help, he tends to forget his own gnawing urge; his problem is solved by a glorious application of the principle of indirection. All who are in Alcoholics Anonymous set great store by the Twelve Steps, but they emphasize the final step which reads: "Having had a spiritual awakening as the result of these steps, we tried to carry this message to alcoholics, and to practice these principles in all our affairs." Here is something very close to the kingdom, for it combines both witness and missionary zeal and redemptive love. It must be noted that all of the Twelve Steps are listed not as admonitions of what men ought to do, but rather as factual accounts of what has been done. This group of principles is not a counsel of perfection but a record of achievement.

While the main contribution to the idea of the Church which Alcoholics Anonymous provides is that of the fellowship of mutual caring, this is not its only contribution. Another, of only slightly less importance, is the insistence on anonymity. Individual notoriety and fame are simply no part of the movement. Here the contrast with the existent Church is sharp and terrible, for almost every branch of the contemporary Church has its dignitaries. The Church in general sets great store by titles, and clergymen are perhaps more open to the dangers of egocentric pride than are members of other professions. Clergymen are one professional group in which the existence of the receiving line of complimentary fans is an accepted practice. One can hardly look at the church page of a metropolitan newspaper on any Saturday without embarrassment and shame, because one is forced to face the fact that the contemporary Church often exhibits the opposite of the true humility which is anonymity. In nearly every city the cult of personal leadership seems to be as blatant in Christian circles as in any others. We are like the worldly societies against which Christ warned specifically. "You know," He said, "that the rulers of the Gentiles lord it over them, and their great men exercise authority over them. It shall not be so among you" (Matthew 20:25-26). These trenchant words can apply just as much to the authority of a local pastor concerned with his own prestige as to papal authority.

Nothing could be more effective, in the effort to rediscover the true pattern of the Church as a loving community, than a serious acceptance of the lesson of the washing of the feet of the disciples. It is hard to understand why nearly all kinds of Christians have tried to be very careful to keep up a perpetual observance of the Last Supper, while only a few groups have been equally concerned with foot washing. The paradox is the greater when we reflect upon the fact that the command of Christ about foot washing is far less equivocal than is any supposed command about the Eucharist.

Some modern Christians are shocked when they first realize that the Four Gospels do not, at any point, represent Christ as commanding a perpetual performance of the Last Supper. The one supposed command (Luke 22:20) does not appear in the best texts. The Revised Standard Version prints the rejected sentence only in a footnote. The Fourth Gospel represents Christ as making no emphasis at all upon the acted parable of bread and wine but, instead, places the entire stress on the washing of the feet.

The present necessity is not that of the establishment of the practice of ceremonial foot washing, though we may be glad that the Brethren and a few others make this particular witness; the point now is the attempt to recover in our Chrisian fellowship the reality of which the foot washing is a powerful symbol. We need to contemplate the present applicability of an act which combines humility and loving service, which renounces unequivocally all struggles for prestige and pre-eminence, and which indicates the radical nature of the break that must be exhibited between the standards of the Church and the standards of the world.

All through our nearly two thousand years of Christian experience there have been recurrent attempts of men and women, who have caught a glimpse of the radical nature of the Christian demand, to answer it by separation from the world. The easiest way to accept the principle of unlimited liability for one another in a Christian society is to retire from the world and to create a little isolated community where all belongs to all. Herein lies the current appeal of semimonastic communities such as the Bruderhof. While it is not hard to see the appeal of these experiments to those who feel the pull of the Christian dream, we must also understand the dangers involved in them. Indeed, the dangers are so great that they seem to outweigh any possible advantages of such experiments in community living. Their basic evil, from the Christian point of view, is that such societies deliberately take their leaven out of the very lump where it is so sorely needed. It is far better to make the Church a society which is *in* the world, demonstrating principles of mutual liability which are in marked contrast *to* the world.

How far should a Church go in the direction of acceptance of mutual responsibility? Should a gifted youth of the Church, whose family is in poverty, be sent to college at the expense of his fellow members? Should the Church match modern business corporations in providing for old age when there is no other provision? Should a Christian couple be able to face the possibility of their sudden death with the calm assurance that the Church of which they are a part will support their orphaned children up to maturity? Unless we know answers to questions as specific as these we do not know very much about the quality of love which the Christian society is meant to exhibit in concrete practice. General statements about love are not adequate.

It has been by a fine instinct, on the part of Christians in various generations, that we have adopted so many names in which the stress has been on love rather than on mere doctrine. Among the names known to all are "Brethren of the Common Life," "Brethren in Christ," "United Brethren," "Society of Brothers," and "Religious Society of Friends." It is thrilling to know that some of the finest fellowships have been formed on the basis of common need, such as those of divorced persons, of ex-prisoners, of released mental patients, and of parents of subnormal children. Wherever there is human tragedy there is a chance for real *koinonia,* the New Testament word for the fellowship of caring. If the Church understands its character, and therefore its business, it will always watch for ways in which affection based upon common need can become redemptive. It is obvious that we have merely scratched the surface in such undertakings. We have around us many new frontiers, but the most unexplored of all frontiers is that of loving fellowship. Too often the existent Church seems only to be a caricature of what a truly caring society would be. But when we have even a brief glimpse of this largely unexplored land we are touched at the deepest point and recognize that this is where true life is to be found.

What the contemporary Church must consider carefully is not *that* it must be a loving fellowship, but *how* it can be such a fellowship. We know that if we are to be worthy of our calling we must go beyond the stiff formality of Sunday morning worship, however valuable that may be, and also beyond the rather thin cordiality of the secular luncheon club or its churchly counterparts. One solution is the formation of small groups—though they, like any human effort, can fail. It is sometimes forgotten that the Sunday School, which is still a potent factor, particularly in certain regions, provides a structure for innumerable small fellowships which are sometimes genuine. Thus the young adult class can become an actual Christian unit, not only engaging in a careful study of the Prophets of Israel or some similar topic, but also performing in the fellowship of caring. A unit of this kind may perform untold acts of mercy of which the captious critic tends to be wholly ignorant.

At no point is the need of redemptive fellowship more pressing than in connection with the problem of race. In countless towns and cities white people and colored people, though often sharing a common Lord, live in worlds as far apart as if they were on different continents. They have different social groups, different clubs, different places for vacations, different places of worship. They must be brought together so that they can know each other, not merely in the already accepted pattern of employer and employee, where the ground rules are well known, but in situations in which the chief consideration is *personal* rather than occupational. There ought to be relations in which, instead of a sharp distinction between benefactor and recipient, there is a mutual sharing. Where is this to be found?

The poor maligned society, the Church, really offers our best hope for the kind of "meeting" without which the race question will not be solved at all. It cannot be solved merely on a political basis. It may, eventually, be solved on a religious basis, provided we truly accept the Judeo-Christian affirmation that God is the Father of all and accepts all with equal love and care. We do not need to assert that all people have equal powers or capabilities; all that we need to assert is that, in the light of Christ, all people are equally *valued* by the Living God. Our ultimate fellowship is therefore derivative.

Too often people suppose, when we talk about a Christian approach to the race problem, that we refer primarily to Negro people attending "white" church services. The fact that this always comes up in discussion is only one more indication of our tendency to think of Sunday morning religion as the heart of Christianity, which it emphatically is not. Indeed, it is one of the major emphases of this book that our present satisfaction with church*going* is a sign of weakness rather than of strength. Naturally we must hold that all places of worship, in Christ's name, must be open to all seekers, but many Negroes may not want to attend public worship with a predominantly white congregation. Why should they? Even if they do attend, this does not necessarily deepen the fellowship. Fellowship does not arise primarily from the fact that people happen to sit on the same benches.

Something far more important than interracial worship is the formation of interracial fellowship groups. These can be formed anywhere, even in the deepest South, and they can be revolutionary in their effect. They should not be organized for the discussion of the race question but for human "meeting." A group composed equally of Americans of African ancestry and Americans of European ancestry can gather to pray, to study, to witness, to share their problems, to plan for the betterment of the world around them. In this way people who have lived for years in the same city as strangers, even though employed in the same places, may become actual *friends*. Their motto may be the words of Christ when He said, "No longer do I call you servants . . . ; but I have called you friends" (John 15:15).

One of the most redemptive of all moves is that in which we make a real effort to see persons as *persons*—and not as our servants or masters or teachers or students or steppingstones for our own progress. The real world is the personal world, and this is where all of the major problems are to be found. It is not really very hard to deal with mere things—partly because they stay put, partly because they are not free, but chiefly because they do not sin. Things are not complicated by pride and struggle for power and the desire to impress, but persons are; and they are, regardless of whether they are white or colored. The real world of our human experience is the complex world of salesmen, waiters, lawyers, doctors, newscasters, advertisers, writers, laborers, bus riders, all trying to get along, all trying to get ahead, and all concerned, by necessity, with one another, whether they like it that way or not. Each makes a difference to every other person in his orbit. In a sense, each is a physician to somebody; each is a salesman; each is a pastor and teacher. This complex world of human relations is the world in which the life of the Church is tested. If it does not win here, what it does anywhere else is of little significance.

The reason for the crucial importance of love is the importance of persons. They provide us with our major joys as well as our major frustrations and our major problems. The world of matter is intrinsically passive, but in a world of persons there are always surprises. The laboratory experiment will work if the conditions are carefully established, but it is not so with persons. We must love, but we are never certain of love in return, for we can never know in advance how the other person will respond. But however difficult the problems of personality may be, it is in the network of personal relations that reality is most fully revealed to us. This is why love, rightly understood as unconditional caring, is truly the greatest thing in the world. We try to be brilliant, but in our best moments we know that there is something better than brilliance, and we know what it is.

There are millions of people waiting for the demonstration of love in action, if only they can find where it is. This is where we need to place the emphasis today, and this is where we need a new theology. The now old-fashioned neo-orthodoxy was needed once, but it has played its role. Whatever antidote to liberal naïvete about human nature was required has been provided. All of us now believe in the universality of human sin; that point no longer needs to be made. Now, in order to keep the balance which loyalty to truth requires, it is wise to recognize that in the human heart, in addition to greed and pride, there is a vast yearning to give ourselves to what is really worthy. The best contemporary spokesman for this new antidote is that continually vital man, Albert Schweitzer:

Our humanity is by no means so materialistic as foolish talk is continually asserting it to be. Judging by what I have learnt about men and women, I am convinced that there is far more in them of idealist will-power than ever comes to the surface of the world. Just as the water of the streams we see is small in amount compared to that which flows underground, so the idealism which becomes visible is small in amount compared with what men and women bear locked in their hearts, unreleased or scarcely released. To unbind what is bound, to bring the underground waters to the surface: mankind is waiting and longing for such as can do that.[9]

It is conceivable that if the Church declines in influence there may still be some philanthropy. Indeed, it existed in the classic pre-Christian society, and it might continue to exist for a while if the Christian roots of philanthropy should wither, but the chance of the emphasis on love and charity being as great without the inspiration of the Church is truly slight. Often, people in the modern world forget the spiritual origin of their own compassion or that of others. Many, for example, greatly admire the medical work of Albert Schweitzer without fully recognizing the Christian character of his motivation. Schweitzer is in Africa because he is in the Company of the Committed and for no other reason. He has told us in his autobiographical books, particularly in *On the Edge of the Primeval Forest,* exactly what the nature of his motivation was and is. He is in Africa because he is an emissary of Jesus Christ and a member of Christ's task force. He might have gone for some other reason, but the truth is that he did not.

Many who know by heart the words of John Donne beginning "no man is an island" and reaching a climax with "send not to ask for whom the bell tolls" fail to realize that these powerful words are part of a sermon, but they thereby miss much of the point. The truncated form of the expression, which is the title of Hemingway's novel, is arresting, but it is not wholly meaningful except in the full Christian setting which the gifted Donne knew how to provide. In any case, it is true that the kind of human concern Donne's words

---

[9] *Out of My Life and Thought* (New York: Holt, Rinehart and Winston, Inc., 1933), p. 114.

express is more likely to arise from the ongoing life of the Church than from any other source. It is from within the life of the Church that the idea of the fellowship of those who bear the mark of pain has arisen.

We have, today, a great deal of philanthropy which is financed and directed by states or cities, but that does not make the continuing witness of the Christian company unnecessary. There are at least two things which members of Christian congregations should do about works of compassion. In the first place, members should move, whenever possible, into public philanthropic work in order to help keep it from becoming increasingly less personal and more bureaucratic. In the second place, Christians, who know what the criterion of validity is, must always be working on the growing edge, starting new experiments. Later the state or city may take over, but often the Church must do the pioneer work, and then let go.

Somewhere in the world there should be a society consciously and deliberately devoted to the task of seeing how love can be made real and demonstrating love in practice. Unfortunately, there is really only one candidate for this task. If God, as we believe, is truly revealed in the life of Christ, the most important thing to Him is the creation of centers of loving fellowship, which in turn infect the world. Whether the world can be redeemed in this way we do not know, but it is at least clear that there is no other way.